Penguin Special s183

Tenants in Dang

Audrey Harvey was born in London, spent ten
years at boarding school, read English at Oxford,
but has been, she says, chiefly educated in the
dock area of East London, where she has been
handling housing problems since 1954. She has
been writing about housing and homeless
families in the *New Statesman* since 1957, has
contributed to *The Times* and the *Observer*, and
has broadcast and appeared on television. Her
Fabian pamphlet *Casualties of the Welfare
State* was published in 1960.

Audrey Harvey has worked on the editorial
staff of a publishing firm and in a shop, a
hospital, and a factory, and she has been a
tenant, a one-house landlord, and an owner-
occupier. She is married to an osteopath, has
one daughter, and lives in Hampstead.

Tenants in Danger

Audrey Harvey

 Penguin Books

Penguin Books Ltd, Harmondsworth, Middlesex, England
Penguin Books Inc., 3300 Clipper Mill Road, Baltimore 11, Md, U.S.A.
Penguin Books Pty Ltd, Ringwood, Victoria, Australia

First published 1964

Copyright © Audrey Harvey, 1964

Made and printed in Great Britain
by C. Nicholls & Company Ltd
Set in Monotype Plantin

Contents

Introduction

The 'wicked landlord' has for years been thought of as an out-dated figure – a character belonging to Victorian melodrama or a Dickens' novel and a butt for music-hall jokes in our grand-parents' or great-grandparents' time. His background was the darkest of slums from which he drew immense wealth and out of which he regularly threw blameless tenants into the snow – their destination invariably being the workhouse.

Although many of these workhouses still stand and homeless people still have to go to them for shelter, all the rest has long seemed part of the disgraceful past. If there are homeless people, it is, we are told by the property-owners' organizations, chiefly due to the continued existence of rent control which allows people selfishly to 'squat' in houses too big for them; while in other cases tenants have no doubt failed to pay their rent or have brought homelessness on their own heads by misbehaving in some other way. But this does not quite tally with what for the past year we have been reading in the papers about the be-haviour of a certain type of landlord.

In fact, the 'wicked landlord' has never really disappeared (he is called 'unscrupulous' now), nor could he be expected to do so. For property is inseparable from power, and rented property is inseparable from power over other people's lives, and that sort of power tends to have a most unfortunate effect on the person who wields it as anyone knows who has ever let a house.

From time to time in the history of rented housing, the really grasping landlord has behaved so badly and proved such a menace to society that he has had to be subjected to controls. And during the Second World War, and for twelve years after it he was obliged for this reason to play a comparatively minor backstage part. Now, with much of his power restored, he has reappeared – but with a difference. He is no longer recognizable as a landlord in the old and very personal sense, and never admits to being one if he can help it, preferring to say that he is merely 'in the property business'. At his worst he is a common crook and a confidence trickster. And he is detested by respectable landlords, who would scorn to use his methods, to almost the same degree as he is by his tenants. For he is bringing the whole business of private ownership into disrepute and inviting, in the process, more controls.

This type of landlord is able to escape personal responsibility for what he does because he is usually one of a group: a member of a property company. And this company – which, in turn, is probably one of a large group formed for the purposes of tax evasion – does not bear his name nor that of any of its other members. It can be registered under any fancy name it chooses and could call itself The Faceless Property Co. or Anonymous Profiteers Inc. if it wanted to be honest. Its official address can be, and often is, merely that of a private house or an office or shop from which letters can be collected or forwarded. The tenants' letters, however, will rarely go any further. If they write making any kind of personal appeal – and so many of them do – their letters will go straight into the waste-paper basket, unanswered. In some cases they have been quite openly told as much.

Another characteristic of this type of landlord is that he is far too clever to break the law. He gets round it instead, by tricking or intimidating helpless people who get in his way. He does not of course do this dirty work himself but employs unscrupulous agents who may, nevertheless, have deceptively 'good' addresses. In any difficulty the landlord can blame the agent for going beyond his instructions, or the agent can just as conveniently throw full responsibility back on the landlord, for whom, he may claim, he is nothing more than a go-between. Tenants who try to fight their way unaided through these defensive barricades usually get nowhere extremely fast.

The aims of this kind of landlord – whose numbers are quite unknown and who has many small-scale private imitators – can be achieved, if he plays his cards skilfully enough, without having to use violence. In any case he is, as a type, far too cautious to hire anyone to use strong-arm methods for him, or to go in for such practices as taking the roof off a house where the lawful tenants are sitting tight. For as a man of business, responsible to his shareholders, what he most fears is a public scandal and involvement with the police. There are, of course, some notorious exceptions – and not only in London. But these are lone wolves operating on their own without any attempt at concealment. In fact they usually do so under their own names – which, to their tenants, are very much household words.

The publicity given to the Rachman property scandals had one particularly useful result. There can now hardly be anyone in this country who is still unaware that all sorts of tricks are being used by the worst landlords (to the horror of the best) to get tenants out of their lawful homes if these could afterwards be relet at much higher rents.

As long as we have decontrolled – or uncontrolled – rents in privately owned rooms, flats, and houses, this will go on full swing. The profits to be made from it are so great and so tantalizing that landlords need to be of very virtuous character if they are to keep their hands entirely clean.

Trickery of this kind has, in fact, been going on throughout the last seven years since the Rent Act came into force, though usually in a quiet way, behind the scenes. Many efforts have been made to expose this publicly. But it took a quite untypical case, that of Rachman, to open the eyes of the general public. For it had very naturally been unwilling, and indeed unable, to believe that the law could possibly be lax enough to allow such practices to go on unchecked.

But even if new laws are passed putting an end to decontrol, thousands of tenants will still be under pressure to leave their homes for a different purpose and one which has always existed: that of selling houses with vacant possession.

However, in the next few years at least, there is not the smallest chance of any government introducing either *total* rent-control or *total* decontrol. The changes to be expected are more of one or more of the other. So the same incentives to get tenants out will continue to exist; and the chief difference will lie in the number of tenants who will find themselves with or without protection against exorbitant rents, and with or without security of tenure.

This affects an enormous number of people. A year or two ago it was estimated that the number of privately rented 'dwellings' (houses, parts of houses, flats, maisonettes, etc.) was between 4 and 4½ million. At the very least that means about 12 million people; and, even so, furnished accommodation has been left out of the reckoning as well as rooms let in houses in which the owners live themselves.

In this uncertain interval, speculation on possible changes in the law affecting security of tenure is naturally at its height. Properties are passing from hand to hand like scorching cakes. Tricks to obtain decontrol or vacant possession are becoming more and more ingenious. And it has seemed that some sort of guide on how to detect and defeat these tricks might be useful. This would have been written long ago but for one great difficulty: it might, before the publication of the Rachman scandals, have had the effect of distributing free tips to wicked landlords.

Tenants who have had threatening letters from their landlords may know exactly what to do and be in a position to do it: they can simply lift the telephone and consult their solicitors. But far more often the threatened tenant has no telephone, no solicitor, and no idea at all what to do. He shows the letter to relatives or neighbours, and among these there will probably be one or two who, rather than admit that they are not sure of the right answer, will give the wrong one with a great air of assurance and quite disastrous results.

Perhaps it will help this threatened tenant to be provided with a guide to the information and advisory services, and with details of what they can do to help him and what, if anything, he will have to pay. This begins on page 15. Perhaps, too, he will find it useful to look at the list of danger signs beginning on page 52. Without this he may not even know that he is in danger until it is too late to do anything about it.

In poor districts, where the worst landlords operate and count on ignorance of the law, a tenant who is under pressure to leave his home may mention this to people he knows in responsible positions. In his terrible anxiety he may tell his doctor or his parson; he may ask the advice of a personnel officer at work; he may go to the police or consult his children's headmaster. But it is not at all likely that any of these people will have enough knowledge of the law to be able to tell him whether or not he has any chance of fighting his case. They may not know, either, where he can get free information about this, or even that he needs any. If he has been told by his landlord to get out, common sense suggests that sooner or later he will have to go. But many families have quite needlessly lost their homes – and, later, their children – through getting that kind of answer.

Lack of the simplest and most essential knowledge of tenancy rights is almost unbelievably widespread. It even extends to people dealing, officially or professionally, with the anxieties of hospital patients, with the welfare of old people, with the granting of rent allowances from public funds, with applications for housing, and with the admission of homeless families, children, or old people to institutions. And because it has not been thought necessary to give such key people any training in tenancy law, even if they first qualified professionally at universities, they can be just as unaware that a tenant is being tricked out of his rights as he may be himself.

But deficiency does not end there. It is an astounding fact that no government department or authority is responsible for recording the number of people who are forced to leave their homes, or for collecting information about malpractices by private landlords – and to read the reports of the Ministry of Housing one would think that none occurred. Research on the subject – far and away the worst of all consumer problems – is in its infancy. None was undertaken by the Government before introducing the 1957 Rent Act. Nor was this thought worth an official inquiry until 1963 when the Milner-Holland Committee began investigations, covering London only, which are bound to expose – among other things – an extraordinarily casual attitude on the part of local authorities. In fact, what tenants have to suffer at the hands of private landlords has always been treated as a private matter with which they are expected to deal on their own and as best they can, no matter what their age or capabilities.

This is a ridiculous state of affairs and a dangerous one too. On a practical level it means that threatened tenants very often do not get legal advice at all or get it much too late.

Chapter 1, 'How to get Legal Advice and Information', is

followed by 'How to Detect and Defeat Trickery' with examples, of how the tricks are intended to work. But there are all sorts of special circumstances in which tenants can find themselves cheated, exploited, and intimidated. And I have included some chapters about the repairs racket, about the endurance tests which often have to be faced by people living in furnished rooms or in the same houses as their landlords, and about the quite fantastic situation of people living in overcrowded houses whose reluctant landlords have been under pressure from a local authority to give them notice to quit to get rid of them.

But at this point an already belated warning must be inserted. This book is intended only as a guide, certainly not as a basis for giving legal advice. And some of the information in it applies only to England and Wales. Not only would it be impossible to include all the exceptions and variations which apply to tenants in Scotland, but I have no personal experience of how these affect them. And this experience is essential because there is a great difference between what, according to the law or to common sense, ought to happen and what, in fact, does.

One point must be made very clear. There are, of course, good, honest, and responsible landlords – probably in quite large numbers, by the law of averages – just as there are, without any doubt at all, bad, dishonest, and irresponsible tenants. But this book is not concerned with good landlords because their tenants need no defence, nor is it concerned with bad tenants because no landlord has to put up with them for long. The law is on the side of the property-owner, and heavily so.

That, indeed, is one reason why my sympathies are strongly with the tenant; and another is simply that his home is not his own. For a tenant, there is no real security, whether the law says there is or not. Of course security is the last thing that an independent and adventurous person wants. But it is the first thing that parents and children and old and ill and timid people need. And the terrible thing for a tenant is that, just as the law can bestow a certain amount of security, so it can whip it away again almost overnight.

One of the things which will, I think, emerge from this book is that the tenant whom decontrol has robbed of all security is in a position to be exploited beyond the limit of endurance. In a country which prizes the freedom of the individual, this tenant is a slave. Although on paper he has certain rights, he cannot in practice safely exercise any of them. For he has only two choices: to submit to his landlord's wishes (which may in the worst cases extend to his wife or his daughter) or to submit to eviction. And no one can protect him from that: not the best solicitor taking out-of-court action, not the courts themselves.

To suggest, however, that this tenant will automatically be exploited, even by a property company, would be most unfair. It should be obvious, and probably is, that not all property companies are unscrupulous in their dealings, nor are all wicked landlords members of property companies. They may not even be rich or, for that matter, male. In fact the poor widow who gets so much sympathy because she has had the burden of landlordism thrust upon her by inheritance may be a positive demon in her personal dealings with her tenants.

She may, however, be quite delightfully the reverse. And one of the perils for tenants is that private landlords are so various and unpredictable and that so much depends on their individual character and attitude. Two of the worst landlords I ever came across from the point of view of neglecting their properties were a woman doctor and a retired major, both of whom lived in the country. The doctor preferred the risk of one of her London houses burning down, with two old ladies in it, to replacing some defective electric wiring. She wrote to her tenants telling them in the rudest possible terms to use candles and stop their grumbling. The major, who did not answer his tenants' letters at all, employed as his manager a semi-literate jobbing builder who did no repairs but produced false evidence of having done them. He also regularly laid down the law, or took it into his own hands, without having, he had to admit, the smallest knowledge of it.

In his brilliant and grimly entertaining Fabian pamphlet on leasehold property, Arthur Skeffington M.P. shows that we still license the same kind of feudal robbery by landlords which went on in the Middle Ages since, at the expiry of a lease, a house built by the leaseholder or his father or grandfather, and all the improvements he has made to the land, go to the freeholder 'who has never made the slightest contribution financially or otherwise', and whose own ancestors, no doubt, originally stole the land from the public simply by putting a fence around it.

With so many long leases of various kinds now expiring many unfortunate people are being faced with unpayable sums for repairs and renewals and with the loss of their homes. But the people I most want to reach are those who as yet have no formal contracts with their landlords and could be prevented from signing iniquitous terms, from being diddled and hoodwinked in dozens of other ways and above all from being prised out of their homes for private gain and by unfair means.

Defence against what has aptly been called 'kid-glove Rachmanism' and against that tragic thing, unnecessary homelessness, are the chief aims of this book. But no one can make lists of traps and dangers without becoming aware of their collective significance or without feeling compelled to ask why, in a civilized and rich country, extreme hardship and injustice should be regarded by so many people in high places as if caused by some unalterable law of nature. So what was to have been merely a handbook has inevitably grown (from Chapter 6 onwards) into a discussion about private landlordism and its future – and not least from the point of view of its expense to the public and its embarrassment to supporting governments.

Although I work in East London, S.O.S. inquiries from people in acute landlord trouble have reached me from many other parts of the city and from outside it. In many cases escape by buying anything but a senile, ailing, and undersized house is remote; in most even this is out. And I have taken a horrified look at the conditions for which people pay rent in Scotland and Wales and in industrial cities such as Manchester and Liverpool. So I hope that this book may serve as some sort of record of what tenants of private landlords could and did suffer during what have so far been the blackest seven years in their post-war history: from 1957 to 1964.

1 How to Get Legal Advice and Information

If tenants are to defend themselves they must get expert advice about how they stand and how they could fall.

It is very dangerous for a tenant to try unaided to diagnose his own position out of a book – this one included. People who have gone in for do-it-yourself diagnosing out of, for instance, the government's handbook *The Rent Act and You* have found years later that their conclusions had been hopelessly wrong. One man was found to have paid more rent than his landlord was entitled to charge – the tenancy was rent-controlled – and had been doing this for six years. A tenant can reclaim overpaid rent only for the previous two years. Another man had convinced himself, quite wrongly, that his right to stay on in his home ceased to exist when the house was taken over by a new owner. He and his family were accepted as being genuinely homeless by the local welfare authority.

This same authority, like most others, had no legal adviser at hand when families presented themselves as being homeless or as due soon to become so. It accepted, and still does, a notice to quit as evidence enough; and it classified homeless people according to the reasons that they themselves gave for their eviction. One classification was simply 'landlord wanted house'. No lawyer would ever accept that as a good enough reason, or a notice to quit as necessarily being a death-warrant. Every day of the week people who think their case is hopeless, but who ask advice about it, go home again in the exhilarating knowledge that they are safe. Information can be an instant cure for cancerous anxiety.

If a tenant wants to know what his rights are under the law he should either consult a solicitor direct or, better still, go first to a Citizens' Advice Bureau (addresses in telephone directories or from town halls, police stations, post offices, or public libraries).

The bureaux' service is confidential and free of charge to all comers. The advice offered them is not concerned with what, morally, they ought or ought not to do, but with what they *can* do, in a very practical sense, and with what probable results.

THE LEGAL ADVICE SERVICE

Payment

One of the important advantages of going first to a Citizens' Advice Bureau is that the tenant can find out there which local solicitors will give him advice for a maximum fee of £1 per session, no matter how high his income, or for only 2s. 6d. or free of any charge at all, under the Legal Aid and Advice Act.

Citizens' Advice Bureau workers, who have lists of these solicitors, supplied by the Law Society, are so trained that they can tell the tenant what, if anything, he will have to pay. Also, they will probably make an appointment for him and, while doing so, explain exactly what questions are bothering him. This is a great help to people who are afraid to consult solicitors direct in case they cannot foot the bill, and to people who have a language difficulty, or who need more time than most solicitors can spare to explain what are often very complicated tenancy tangles.

This invaluable means of getting free or very inexpensive legal advice dates from only a few years ago and is not yet nearly well enough known. But it has to be noted that what is given is spoken advice only.

Extra Expenses

If the solicitor finds it necessary not only to give advice but to write letters (for instance, to the tenant's landlord), he may be able to claim the cost under legal aid provision, or he may have to make an extra charge. Many solicitors make no charge at all to their poorest clients, especially if they come through Citizens' Advice Bureaux. But naturally others do; and there is no set scale of charges.

Limitations to the Legal Advice Service

There is as yet no legal aid provision to help a tenant who wants to be represented by a solicitor before a tribunal – for instance a rent tribunal – and who cannot afford the cost. The minimum cost is about £10 but it can be much more. Again, there is no set scale of charges. (But see also Legal Advice Centres, page 23.)

It can also happen that there are no local solicitors who are willing to give advice for £1 or less, per session. Or the tenant may need advice in a hurry when a single-handed solicitor, who could have helped him, is either in court or has no free appointments for a week. In poor districts the number of solicitors, especially those taking legal aid cases, is ridiculously small.

Sometimes solicitors could very usefully apply to the courts for immediate restraint orders against landlords allegedly guilty of threatening or violent behaviour, or against those who have unlawfully locked tenants out. But often the tenant cannot afford the cost, and it is more difficult to get emergency legal aid for taking an action in the courts than for defending one. The evidence is often harder to substantiate, the outcome is therefore less predictable, and the State is more chary of risking its money.

LEGAL HELP FROM THE CITIZENS' ADVICE BUREAUX

But if a tenant consults a Citizens' Advice Bureau he can still get the information he so often needs very urgently.

Most Citizens' Advice Bureaux have their own honorary legal advisers (solicitors or barristers) who can be contacted by telephone. And, at any rate, a C.A.B. worker who has worked in close cooperation with solicitors for years (and has been brought many more tenancy problems than ever come the way of any one solicitor) will in many cases be able to give the information single-handed.

Also, certain people would rather take no action at all than go to a solicitor because they see this as eventually involving an appearance in court or are convinced that solicitors will take their last penny from them. So a C.A.B. is often as far as a tenant will go.

Value of the Bureaux' Experience

Some people may very naturally feel that no one except a qualified lawyer should ever give advice on what, strictly, are legal problems, although solicitors' clerks frequently do this and so do information officers at town halls.

But one of the chief purposes of Citizens' Advice Bureaux is to *explain* legislation of all kinds so that people can understand their rights and obligations. And there is a special reason for their knowledge of tenancy rights.

Before solicitors were able to provide their own free, or very inexpensive, advisory service, C.A.B. workers had to fill the gap with the help of their own legal advisers. And as this gap was still there by the time the Rent Act came into force, and for two years afterwards, many of them became experts through sheer necessity and a great deal of day-to-day practice.

How the Bureaux Can Help

The C.A.B. service acts as an essential intermediary between the public and the authorities. A tenant can find it very useful that his Bureau can put his case for him to the local public health department, if his home is in bad repair; or to the National Assistance Board if he cannot pay his rent because he cannot work. (And, for that matter, it can, of course, also put this to his landlord if he is at all approachable.)

There is also growing cooperation between bureaux and local M.P.s. And people in tenancy difficulties are often referred to the Bureaux by doctors, solicitors, local councillors, rent tribunal officers, and, occasionally, after a case has come to court, by judges.

There are no limits to this kind of cooperation. But there is another kind which benefits tenants in a less direct way. The Bureaux are increasingly asked to help with housing research, private and public. They have provided reports on the causes of homelessness, on every conceivable aspect of private landlordism, on hardship connected with increased rates, and so on. They are frequently consulted, too, by the broadcasting and television authorities and by the press. Although names and addresses are never given, as a matter of the strictest principle, all this helps to expose hardship and injustice in a general way. And because the Bureaux are scattered all over the country, it also helps to show that the worst tenancy abuses are by no means confined to any one area, such as Notting Hill, or city, but exist wherever an extensive shortage of housing does.

Perhaps the most important form of cooperation, from the tenant's point of view, is that between the C.A.B. service and the Ministry of Housing. Since the service was set up, during the war, the Ministry has found the Bureaux increasingly useful for explaining to the public any new housing Act, for reporting back difficulties – and, occasionally, for predicting them beforehand. But the provisions of the Rent Act were so immensely complicated that, for the first time, the Ministry was obliged publicly to advise bewildered tenants (and landlords) to consult their local Bureaux if they could not afford to consult solicitors.

In fact the C.A.B. service – which enjoys the confidence of the Law Society – has become the only one of all the non-legal social services which is equipped both to deal with tenancy problems and abuses and to make them known.

Also, this service, as well as being free, is non-political and impartial and takes on all comers no matter what their income or status. For instance, it is often consulted by small-scale landlords, as well as by tenants. And because of the great number of people using the service for housing problems alone, Bureau workers naturally become very knowledgeable not only about local housing conditions, but about which landlords or agents are dubious or worse in their dealings, and also about which solicitors such landlords use.

Naturally a tenant who is under pressure from his landlord will benefit from this kind of knowledge, and so will his eventual legal adviser, to whom it will be passed on. It can also happen that a Bureau has a few wicked landlords – minor operators of course – on its books; and they not infrequently stop ill-treating their tenants after being warned about the risk of, for instance, control orders being made on their properties.

Help With Inexperienced Landlords

Landlords reported to be behaving with what appears to be complete ruthlessness to their tenants often turn out to be fools or dupes rather than knaves, especially if they are newcomers to this country.

They may be behaving just as their own landlords did to them when they themselves were tenants, perhaps assuming that in this country this is the normal thing to do. Often they have been advised by the agents selling houses to them that as soon as they take over they can push all the protected tenants (with controlled rents) out. They may have bought their houses at vacant possession prices on this very understanding. When they find that these agents have exploited their ignorance, their bitterness can be imagined. Sometimes a C.A.B. can deflect violent intentions and reduce landlord-and-tenant animosities simply because it provides a place where grievances can be aired and steam let off. But the Bureaux always try to avoid having dealings with both landlord and tenant in any one case.

Help for Elderly Tenants

Most of the people who still have 'protected' or rent-controlled tenancies are now, for all sorts of reasons which will be gone into later, old or at least elderly, in poor circumstances, and not very well aware of their rights or able to act for themselves. Yet they are sitting targets for landlords bent on gaining vacant possession by trickery. A C.A.B. can be particularly useful in detecting this at an early stage.

Helping the Tenant's Solicitor

It helps a busy solicitor considerably if the position of the tenant he is going to advise can first be disentangled, if certain essential information can be found out for him from the local rates office, and if the tenant is reminded to bring with him his old and current rent books, plus any letters from his landlord or agent. Where rents are controlled calculations are often needed to see that they are not being overcharged – a job at which many solicitors jib – while matters concerning national insurance and national assistance are rather outside their sphere. But they are well inside the sphere of a C.A.B. and they can vitally affect a tenant's ability to pay his rent. In fact there are situations in which the tenant of decontrolled property can be virtually forced into rent arrears (see page 50 for details). If a C.A.B. is not too feverishly pressed for time it will supply tenants with figures and facts to take to their solicitors.

Letters to Landlords and Agents

C.A.B. workers are very often asked to draft or write necessary letters to landlords or agents for threatened tenants with apparently wicked landlords.

It is surprising how much mere letters can do to counter trickery. The whole point of writing them is to call the landlord's bluff or make him aware that what he is doing has been detected. So the best approach is to ask, for instance, on what grounds a tenant has been issued with a new rent book marked 'decontrolled' when he appears to have a controlled tenancy; or what has been the purpose of suggesting that his rights do not still exist although the property has changed hands; or under what provision of the Rent Act his rent has been increased; or whether it can be taken that he will be provided with a very long lease to cover his loss of protective rights if he moves to other accommodation (or simply upstairs) as the landlord has suggested.

These questions, which involve no laying down of the law, can hardly cause offence if the landlord is innocent or ignorant. But if he is neither, he will not find it easy to reply without incriminating himself.

These are the sort of questions that anyone can put to his landlord. But when they are asked by a Citizens' Advice Bureau, with reference to its legal adviser, they naturally carry much more weight, and will at once put the landlord on his guard. In nine out of ten cases the tenant is afterwards left in peace and at his proper rent. And the Bureau either hears nothing, or is told that the notice to quit has been withdrawn, or that the whole thing was due to a clerical mistake.

This letter-writing service is enormously appreciated and because it is so effective tenants feel that, here, they have got a real means of defence.

Discovering Threatened Tenants

There is a final reason, and a very powerful one, why the Bureaux are useful in countering trickery. Because they deal with every sort of question, an inquirer may come about something quite other than landlord trouble – perhaps hire purchase, or income tax, or divorce; and while discussing his finances, he is sure to mention what he has to spend on rent. That alone can be a clue.

On the other hand a man who comes, say, about being sacked without notice from his job may mention that his present address will not find him next week, as he and his family have got to get out. He may have no idea that, just possibly, his notice to quit is not valid. A great many intended evictions have also been nipped in the bud through people coming to a Bureau to ask where they can store furniture, or whether furniture on H.P. can be moved from one address to another, or whether the National Assistance Board helps with fares to go to another town, or how to find a moneylender.

Incidentally, C.A.B.s have no funds for helping people in emergencies. Nor is there any official provision elsewhere for immediate loans of small sums to prevent homelessness. Yet sums of under £10 can often remove an otherwise insuperable obstacle – for instance that of having to produce a week's rent in advance for a vacant room found after a very long and exhausting search. And very often homeless people have not got enough money left for a meal to give them enough energy to go on searching, let alone for fares or telephone calls.

Difficulties in the Citizens' Advice Bureau System

Many people may object that they have no Citizens' Advice Bureau anywhere near them, or that the local Bureau is open for only a few days a week for a few hours, or that the workers do not do more than give information. In many places some or all of this is true. The reasons are complicated. One of them is that, in spite of being used by many government departments, this is a voluntary organization. It is largely, by no means wholly, run by unpaid workers most of whom can only work part-time. In addition, the Bureaux are directly responsible only to local committees. Of course there is a parent body: the National Council of Social Service. But its function is chiefly to advise, to organize, and to feed the Bureaux with accurate and up-to-date information, rather than to direct their activities in any detail.

However, by far the most important reason for deficiencies is the complete dependence of the Bureaux for money on local sources – chiefly local authorities (in London, borough councils) some of whom are generous, some quite astoundingly the reverse. This will be discussed in Chapter 8.

The C.A.B. system has its drawbacks, but they are eminently curable. And if that system were radically changed the service would lose not only its invaluable independence as a go-between but its ability (which a local authority service could not share) to treat inquiries in absolute confidence. For instance, inquirers do not even have to give their names, and no action is taken without their approval. Also, if a service is to be approachable by even the most timid people, a little informality is a great advantage.

If people want a C.A.B. in their district the thing to do is to ask the local authority to set one up – and to support it properly.

LEGAL ADVICE CENTRES

The wretched term 'poor men's lawyers' is on the way out. It refers to lawyers who give advice voluntarily at C.A.B.s and legal advice centres. There are legal advice centres of various kinds, where solicitors can be consulted, in certain big towns and cities. They can be very useful because they operate in the evenings. Those which do not get a supporting grant, and are run voluntarily by solicitors, make their own rules about the kind of cases they can handle and about charges for legal advice (not usually more than 2s. 6d.) and for legal representation in court if this is undertaken – such charges being only a fraction of the normal cost.

Because new centres of this kind open, and old ones shut,

rather often addresses are best got from Citizens' Advice Bureaux or information offices at town halls.

One of the most useful functions of the centres is to cover gaps in legal aid provision. For instance the grant-supported centres can get a client who has passed a means test represented before a rent tribunal for only £2 4s. 6d.

A fairly common disadvantage, however, is that people have to wait too long for too short a consultation with a rather inexperienced solicitor.

INFORMATION OFFICES

Local authorities often provide their own information services. In London these authorities are borough councils. Some prefer to do this rather than help to support a Citizens' Advice Bureau – and that can be the reason why there may be no Bureau in that area. Some authorities, however, do both. But where this happens, the grant to the Citizens' Advice Bureau can be inadequate for that reason alone.

The ground that an information office can cover is naturally rather limited, and because it represents authority it has to be cautious in taking action. Also, there are certain problems which tenants would not take to a town hall department, either because they do not want their private affairs known there or because they need the help of an independent and impartial service for the very purpose of putting their case to the local authority.

Information officers are usually very knowledgeable and go much further in helping people than might be expected – especially people with tenancy problems, on which many of them have become expert.

LEGAL ADVICE POSTAL SERVICES

These are provided by certain newspapers and are run by solicitors and barristers. Thousands of people write to them for advice and what they get is of an excellent standard. But the difficulties of advising on tenancy problems by post are obvious: everything depends on the tenant being able to state his own case and to provide all the information needed to diagnose it; and that is exactly what, usually, he cannot do.

MEMBERS OF PARLIAMENT

M.P.s run their own very valuable advisory services in their 'surgeries' or local committee rooms for any of their constituents who make appointments to consult them there. Not all M.P.s, of course, are experts on housing. It is a matter of great luck for local people if this happens to be so, and if the M.P. is an active one. But a threatened tenant cannot usually wait to see his M.P., and he may feel chary of consulting him for political reasons.

TENANTS' ASSOCIATIONS

This is a very useful and rapidly growing service. The most efficient tenants' associations make use of the legal and advisory services in their areas, or have their own legal advisers and do not try to handle life-and-death emergencies on their own.

Some of them use their local Citizens' Advice Bureaux. In fact, a single Bureau may be consulted by three or four local associations representing thousands of tenants. Members of Parliament are often consulted by them too, and so are local councillors.

As a service, a tenants' association can be helpful in a special way to old or disabled or ill people who cannot leave their homes to get professional advice. Many associations make it their business to call on old people to ask if they are in any landlord trouble. If they are, the association then acts as their representative. And, incidentally, it is not at all uncommon to refuse to take membership fees from people dependent on pensions.

Many cases of intimidation by landlords would never be discovered and fought but for this active concern for helpless people by the associations. Theirs is the only service which can and does search for people in difficulty or danger, rather than wait for them to present themselves.

The associations, as a collection of private individuals, have the advantage of complete freedom of action. And the banding together of tenants to resist pressures, and to use the power of the press and of broadcasting to show up offending landlords, can be tremendously effective. It also involves far less chance of retaliation than the unsupported tenant has to fear.

(Landlords, of course, have their own very powerful associations: the National Federation of Property Owners and the Property Owners Protective Association, which now have a joint council.)

*

Nothing is more certain than that most people still have no idea that all these services exist, let alone what sort of work they do. None of them is properly publicized. But in some areas either they do not exist, or not all of them do, or they may be of a poor standard, or are not available at the times when they are needed most. It is of enormous importance that this should be put right. What is at stake is, in one word, justice.

2 How to Detect and Defeat Trickery

There are innumerable people in responsible jobs who could help enormously to fight tenancy trickery if they knew on what grounds to suspect it.

I am thinking of people in every branch of the social services: doctors, nurses, teachers; people in offices dealing with health, housing, rates, and even income tax; with anything to do with children, old people, marriage, divorce, birth, death, debt, insurance, pensions, unemployment, sickness, or national assistance. For these often find themselves consulted by worried people whose terror of losing their homes naturally weighs on their minds to the exclusion of everything else.

I am thinking, too, of bank managers and of employers; of the sociologist who, while investigating something quite else, receives all sorts of anxious confidences about housing troubles – just as journalists do, and as everyone does whose job involves going into other people's homes. This list could be added to endlessly because wherever people meet for discussions, public or private, political or otherwise – on almost any social subject – housing will crop up.

Those who simply want to know what trickery clues to look out for, so that they can urge the people concerned to take expert advice at the earliest possible moment, will find a list of danger signs beginning on page 52.

But many professional people would probably prefer to be on rather firmer ground, so that they can explain to people who consult them why they are in danger, exactly how and with what purpose they are being tricked, whether a notice to quit can be fought, and what advantages there can be in playing for time.

*

The people most subject to trickery – with a view to getting them out – are, obviously, those whose rents cannot lawfully be raised above certain limits and who possess security of tenure – which means, very roughly, security against having to leave their homes simply because this would suit their landlords.

Such tenants are very sharp thorns in any speculative landlord's flesh although they are by no means unprofitable. The rents they pay, especially in London, are often higher than those paid for council flats, even if their homes have no conveniences at all. But of course they are very much lower than the rents that the landlord could charge if there were no restrictions.

These people are often referred to as 'protected tenants' or as 'statutory tenants' (although this is not legally accurate) and the processes used by unscrupulous landlords to oust them is now known as 'de-statting'. This process can take a whole variety of extremely cunning and unpleasant forms, and examples will be given later in this chapter and throughout the book.

*

The people least *subject to trickery* – for ousting purposes – are, just as obviously, those whose rents can be raised without limit and who have no security of tenure – except the four weeks to which every tenant became entitled under the 1957 Rent Act. They can of course be cheated and exploited, especially over repairs, but that is another matter (see page 71).

The people in this second category are those with *genuine decontrolled tenancies*.

THE IMPORTANCE OF ESTABLISHING WHETHER A TENANCY IS CONTROLLED OR DECONTROLLED

If the tenant has not brought his rent book with him or has not got one to bring, the best and by far the safest way of setting out to answer this all-important question is to start by assuming that his tenancy may be decontrolled. This is comparatively easy to establish quickly and with certainty.

There are one or two very good reasons for starting this way. If the tenancy is found to be decontrolled, any suspicions that the tenant is being tricked into paying more rent than he can lawfully be charged can then be instantly ruled out.

For instance, a rent charge of £6 per week for a couple of dank basement rooms, plus a key money demand, in cash, of £100 may well look like trickery. But if the tenancy is genuinely decontrolled under the law, these charges will represent exploitation, not trickery; for the landlord of decontrolled property (let for less than 21 years) can charge what he likes without breaking or getting round the law. And he can also get a blameless tenant evicted on the sole ground that his notice to quit has expired. (But see also pages 34, 42, 55, 93, 96, and 97.)

HOW TO SPOT A DECONTROLLED TENANCY
Warning

The tests given below are valid only as long as the 1957 Rent Act remains in force and unaltered.

Any big change in tenancy law affecting security of tenure always has to be widely publicized to avoid complete chaos. If and when this happens, the tests in this book will no longer apply. Probably a government handbook will be issued, and that should be used instead – or inquiries should be made from information or advisory offices, or direct from solicitors (see Chapter 1).

Whatever changes are made in the next few years, one thing is certain: both rent-controlled and decontrolled tenancies will still continue to exist, although in a different proportion. To clamp controls on every kind of accommodation would mean great hardship to landlords letting furnished rooms in their own houses, and great difficulty for people needing a temporary place to live; while to remove all controls would produce the same kind of chaos which resulted in New York when this was tried in 1946.

This means that 'de-statting', which went on before the Rent Act was passed (although on a much smaller scale), will still go on even if it is repealed.

The chief purpose of including tests which will certainly become inapplicable sooner or later is to prevent families from losing their homes unnecessarily in the interval for lack of proper advice. Besides, that interval could be a long one. After the change

of government in 1945 most of the reforms which followed were
not made law for three years. And after the change of government in 1951, the Rent Act did not come into force for six years.

Clearing the Ground

Rent Books. The fact that a tenant may have a rent book with the
word 'decontrolled' written or printed on it is most emphatically
not enough to go on. This in itself can be a trick deliberately used
to deceive him or anyone he may consult.

Furnished and Unfurnished. In order to be sure that a tenancy is
decontrolled under the law, certain quite simple questions have
to be asked.

In setting these questions out I am referring to *unfurnished*
tenancies only, and to those where no charges for services – such
as electricity – are included in the rent.

If there is any doubt about these services, or if the landlord
has provided any furniture at all – however gimcrack or inadequate – or if any room, for instance a kitchen, is shared with
him or with anyone else in the house, the tenant may be able to
get help from a rent tribunal, and he should get advice on this at
once.

The position of the tenant of *furnished accommodation* and the
kind of help he can get from a rent tribunal is discussed in
Chapter 5 (page 95). At present all furnished tenancies are free
from control unless they have come under the control of a rent
tribunal through an application by a tenant, a landlord, or a local
authority.

Special Circumstances. A tenant ought also to get legal advice: if
his tenancy includes a shop, café, workrooms, or offices; if any
land goes with it; if, when he first rented the house, it had been
requisitioned (taken over) by the local council during the war; if
his home goes with a job of any kind; if it is part of a public house;
if the house he lives in was built or converted into flats after
30 August 1954; if a lease of twenty-one years or more is coming
to an end; or if the tenant pays 'ground rent'; if the house is to
be improved with the help of a grant, or closed (temporarily,
partially, or wholly) or demolished or bought – compulsorily or

otherwise; or if the rent has been controlled by a tribunal, even if the rooms were let unfurnished. See also Chapter 3.

To Whom Is Rent Paid? After establishing that the tenancy is unfurnished, that none of the special circumstances mentioned above apply, and that it really is a tenancy (i.e. that rent is being paid for rooms not shared with the landlord, and without an included charge for meals as in the case of lodgers), the next step is to discover to whom the rent is paid.

If the rent is paid to someone other than the owner of the house, or his agent or rent collector, that 'someone' will turn out to be the tenant of the house, or part of the house if it is divided for letting, and the person paying rent to him will be his sub-tenant.

Sub-Tenants. It may be useful to note that a sub-tenant cannot be given notice to quit, or have his rent raised, by the owner of the house. This can be done only by the tenant who, although he may be rather startled to realize it, is his landlord-in-law.

What most people are surprised to learn is that sub-tenants have the same protection as tenants under the law. And this was not affected by the 1957 Rent Act. See also pages 33 and 55.

Further Steps

When Did the Tenancy Start. Now that the ground has been slightly cleared, the first and very important question to ask is this:
1. Did the tenant (or sub-tenant) move into his present home from another address *on or after 6 July 1957?*

If the answer to this is 'Yes', the tenancy is definitely decontrolled and no further questions need be asked. The reason for saying this is that *all* new tenancies were decontrolled under the Rent Act which came into force on 6 July 1957.

(But if the tenant's address has not changed and is still say, 3 Hill Road, NI, but he is now living in a different part of the house, or has got more or fewer rooms, he should be sent for diagnosis to an expert, as this is an extremely dodgy matter.)

But what if the answer to that first question about moving was 'No' and the tenant was in unchanged residence before the Rent Act began to operate? There will be one more question to ask.

Rateable Values.

2. Does the tenant know what the rateable value of his home is?

This is very important because houses and flats with a rateable value of over £40 a year in London* and Scotland (£30 elsewhere) were immediately decontrolled when the Rent Act came into force. However, as there was a revision of rateable values in 1963, what is used for this test is the 'old' rateable value that applied before 1 April 1963 and as far back as 7 November 1956.

If the tenant says he knows the rateable value of his home, he should be asked how he came to know it. It is not safe for him to go by a figure scribbled down for him by his landlord. Even the figures entered on official forms by landlords or their agents are very often inaccurate and have to be sent back for correction.

It is not enough, either, that the tenant has been shown a figure on a rate demand. For the rate demand may cover the whole house, whereas he may occupy only a small part of it. Or the demand may show the new rateable value which will be much higher than the old, and this could easily deceive him.

For example: two houses next to each other in East London both had an 'old' rateable value of £26 a year and were therefore not decontrolled under the Rent Act. They now have a new rateable value of £70 a year although the actual rates have gone down. The tenants, naturally enough, were totally bewildered by this situation and flew into a panic when they got a letter from their landlord suggesting that their tenancies had become decontrolled since the 1963 revaluation, and that he would be providing new tenants with orders to view their homes. It was very hard to convince them that they had not lost their security of tenure – since the 'old' rateable value was the operative one.

Anyone can ring up the rates office of a town hall to find out the 'old' rateable value of a flat or house to help a tenant to diagnose his position. But if his tenancy covers only a part of a house, he will need a separate assessment of the rateable value for that part only. He can get help with this from the local Valuation Officer either direct or through a Citizens' Advice Bureau.

* In the Metropolitan Police district of London. There is a map on the back of the government handbook *The Rent Act and You* showing how far this extends. It is roughly the area covered by the Greater London Council.

The Sub-Tenant's Position. Sub-tenants have to be particularly careful about this, but they often find that they are in a safer position than the tenant of the house. For while the whole house may be decontrolled by this rateable value test, the same result may well not be so in the case of those parts of it which are rented by sub-tenants.

A very unfair situation can therefore arise: the tenant of a decontrolled house can find himself evicted, while his sub-tenants have a right to stay on – a right which remains unchanged even if the property changes hands. For this reason, sub-tenants are even more subject to trickery than tenants are.

All this may sound very complicated and confusing on paper, but it is much less so in practice. Time after time the whole business of making sure that an unfurnished tenancy is genuinely decontrolled is settled by getting a definite 'Yes' in answer to Question 1.

DANGERS TO TENANTS OF DECONTROLLED PROPERTY

The point of making sure about decontrol is not simply that of being able to rule out suspicions based on startlingly high rents. It enables a tenant to be warned that he should very carefully watch his step in all his dealings with his landlord and restrain himself, if humanly possible, from making even the most well-justified complaints.

The reason for saying this is that if the tenant has not been provided with a tenancy agreement, he can be given four weeks' notice to quit, against which the courts have no power to protect him no matter how great his hardship. This is why he cannot be advised to stand on any of his very few rights (such as the right if he pays his rent weekly to be provided with a properly entered rent book) or to question the landlord's treatment of him in any way, or even to complain about insanitary conditions which may be making his children ill. Many tenants, nowadays, get notice to quit for asking the help of the health authorities. One whom I know got notice for refusing to state to a tax officer that his rent was lower than it really was; another for refusing to give false evidence for his landlord against

another tenant; another for asking for a tenancy agreement –
and so on.

Notice to Quit Decontrolled Property

With the worsening of the housing shortage, landlords have been
able to pick and choose their tenants, and to replace those who
displease them in any way. Very often no reason at all is given
for a notice to quit, and none has to be stated on it.

But there is one more point to add here. If a tenant of decontrolled property does get notice to quit he should be referred at
once for professional advice to make sure that the notice is valid
in itself. These notices can be faulty in many ways and frequently
do not allow for the full four weeks to which every tenant and
sub-tenant is entitled – especially if the landlord wants to clear
the house in a hurry.

Advantages of Playing for Time. Where a notice is found to be
faulty at least the tenant is entitled to another four weeks' grace
during which he could just possibly be lucky enough to find
somewhere else to live. Occasionally, too, a landlord can be
induced to relent in the interval. Some small landlords give notice
in a fit of rage which does not last. Some do not like to appear to
the authorities to be making families homeless for no good
reason. Some come to terms with their tenants – though usually
only by the tenant agreeing to pay more rent, or to move into a
smaller room or into fewer rooms, or not to report that the landlord is overcrowding the house or is behaving in some way which
he would rather keep quiet. Sometimes, too, a landlord will give
in if when his notice to quit expires the tenant sits tight. He may
well not want the expense and trouble of going to court for an
eviction order even though – if he makes no mistakes – he is
sure to win and to have costs awarded to him too.

The tenant ought to be warned about these costs. They rarely
come to less than £20 and can be much heavier. The only point
of waiting to be taken to court and of paying up is that more time
will be gained. When the four weeks' notice to quit has expired
there may be another fortnight or more before a summons is
served on the tenant, and it will be at least another month before

the case can be heard. After the hearing, there may be another twenty-eight days to the date on the eviction order. But there will still be an interval before the bailiffs arrive, and there are ways of getting it lengthened.

Most tenants leave their homes when their notices to quit expire because they cannot afford the costs of losing hopeless cases or because there may be no point in staying on. If they have children, low earnings, and no savings, their chances of finding another home, in London at any rate, will be so small that they will have no difficulty in being accepted as genuinely homeless.

But there can be a very good reason for hanging on. No family wants to become homeless unnecessarily just when a baby or an offer of a council flat is due, or while one of the parents is in hospital.

Where there is some point in delaying, it is vitally important to consult a solicitor. He may be able to find some ground for defence. It could easily be that the landlord has spoilt his case by not doing exactly what his own solicitor has advised, or by not telling his solicitor the true facts. If so, the tenant will be, temporarily at least, in a much happier position. He will not be refused legal aid – as he would have been if he had had no defence at all; and will not have to worry about having to pay costs and fees to be represented in court, which he could not have afforded on his own. He will also stand to gain even more time, because a defended case takes longer to get a hearing than an undefended one does. And if the defence succeeds, the landlord will have to start again from the beginning.

Of course the landlord is bound to win in the end if the property is decontrolled. But rather than go through the whole procedure a second time, he may offer the tenant money to leave his home, and this could be handy for a premium on another one.

NOTE Tenants of furnished accommodation may have another means of delaying eviction; see pages 95 f.

Threats

A thwarted landlord may threaten violence. Where this happens, it has been found very useful to give the tenant a letter to show his landlord. This should explain in the plainest language that if there is any attempt to throw the tenant out or injure him in any way, he will certainly sue the landlord and will probably be awarded damages of at least £100. Of course this does not always work. Some landlords simply tear the letters up unread. Others are not worried about losing £100. It works best with a landlord who is ignorant of the law. The fact that the letter is not addressed to him is important. He cannot accuse the writer of interfering in his affairs, but knows that he is under observation.

Action by a solicitor is even more effective. He may write a very strongly worded letter direct to the landlord or apply to the courts for an injunction against him. But there is usually too little time even to get the tenant an appointment with a solicitor.

DANGERS TO PROTECTED OR RENT-CONTROLLED TENANCIES

It is very dangerous for anyone but a solicitor or an expert to assure a tenant that his tenancy is controlled unless this is clearly stated in his *current* rent book or in a letter from his landlord. Certificates of disrepair and other statutory repair forms are useful clues because they are issued to controlled tenants only.

Unfortunately the tenant may not have brought his rent book with him, or he may not have one to bring. And sub-tenants' rent books hardly ever have any information in them of any kind. When this happens, and there is no other evidence, all the clearing of the ground, as described earlier in this chapter, has to be gone through – not forgetting the questions about special circumstances, much less the vitally important rateable value and length-of-tenancy tests. And at the end of all this, there ought to be a second opinion.

How Much Security Does a Protected Tenant Have?

Where a tenancy is quite definitely controlled, it is natural to jump to the conclusion that the tenant has absolute protection under the law against having to leave his home if he does not want to, and that he can therefore only be dislodged by trickery. This is not so.

Claims for Possession. The owner of a rent-controlled house which he bought before 6 November 1956 can claim possession of it if he needs to live in it himself or needs it for his parents or for a son or daughter over the age of eighteen. And a tenant can do much the same to a protected sub-tenant, if he needs more space for his family.

Small-scale trickery sometimes goes on here. For the courts cannot keep track of whether the landlord or his family ever do live in the house if the claim is successful (hardship on either side has to be considered); and there can be just as much un-certainty about whether a tenant taking similar action really needs more space or just wants to get his sub-tenant out, because the house concerned is not inspected. But this is scarcely the kind of trickery that property companies or big-scale landlords can go in for.

Much more important, a landlord can of course claim posses-sion if a protected tenant owes him rent or if he has been sub-letting against the landlord's orders or at an excessive rent, or is overcrowding the house or damaging it or using it for any purpose other than the one originally agreed, or is guilty of 'nuisance', which can cover a variety of sins. This gives only a rough idea of the grounds on which landlords can claim. They can also get controlled tenants out if they themselves have overcrowded a house and are required to put this right by a local authority, or if the accommodation is wanted for an employee of the landlord or if the latter offers 'suitable alternative accommodation (see also page 38).

Because these grounds exist, it is rash to assume that a land-lord who serves a notice to quit on a protected tenant is neces-sarily bluffing or hatching some machiavellian plot. He may be perfectly justified – or he may not.

Not long ago, a great many protected tenants who all had the same landlord (a property company) reported in great indigna-tion that the agents had sent them notices to quit for arrears of rent, although they owed nothing. The agents, when challenged, said that the notices had been sent out indiscriminately – in the hope that some of them would 'hit the mark'. They explained, but without apology, that there had been some confusion in the office because one of their rent collectors had decamped, taking dozens of rent books with him, so that there had been no means of checking them for arrears. It had seemed a good idea to assume guilt, because some reactions might confirm it. One of the notices had been sent to a man who, as a sitting tenant, had bought his house two years before. He decided, much to the satisfaction of his neighbours, to get even with the agents; and he not only let his case go to court undefended, but did not disclose that he was no longer a tenant until the bailiffs came to evict him.

Too often, nowadays, protected tenants are either threatened with legal proceedings or sent notices to quit on grounds which are insufficient for a county court to grant an eviction order.

The solicitors or agents, acting in this way for the landlords, of course know that they are on very shaky ground and will not be able to proceed if the tenant takes advice. The hope is, of course, that he will not have the wit to do so and will be so frightened that he will get out of his own accord. If only one out of ten tenants does this, the rewards to the landlord will be far greater than his solicitor's fees.

There are, however, some cases where the landlord sends with his notice to quit an offer of 'alternative accommodation'.

Offers of Alternative Accommodation. If a landlord has some grounds, but not enough, to get a protected tenant out, he can strengthen his claim by offering him 'suitable alternative accommodation'. He can do this, too, if he has a reasonable need to get the tenant out, perhaps because his house gets in the way of a building project for which the landlord has got official permission.

The word 'alternative' means, roughly, that the tenant would be no worse off if he took the accommodation offered. This was much easier to arrange before the Rent Act came into force. But with all new tenancies decontrolled the tenant would, by moving, lose his security of tenure and his controlled rent and would very obviously be worse off – unless the landlord were to provide him with a very long lease at a very low rent.

These offers must also be reasonable in other ways. Distance from schools and jobs has to be considered, and a tenant could not be expected to move, say, from Hampstead to Hackney against his will.

The fact that these offers come with a notice to quit naturally leads tenants to think that they must be accepted, and they are not, of course, told otherwise.

An offer of alternative accommodation can in certain circumstances be made to a protected tenant without involving the landlord in any difficulty at all and, if accepted, it can bring him great rewards.

The purpose is to get possession of *part* of the tenant's home, often with a view to getting the whole of it later on if his life becomes intolerable. The victims here are almost always old people living alone. The process is perfectly legal but not remarkably ethical. It can involve exploitation of the tenant's ignorance by trapping him into acceptance unawares, and exploitation of his age by the use of harassing tactics.

Here is a current example: An elderly widow who had lived in her small rent-controlled house since the beginning of the First World War and who had the tenancy of the whole of it, recently received a notice to quit from her landlord's solicitor. With it came a very frightening letter accusing her of having broken the terms of her tenancy. It appeared that she had advertised for a lodger and the landlord's agent had seen her advertisement in a local newspaper.

The solicitor sending her that notice was well aware that no court would have granted an eviction order simply on the evidence of an advertisement. It would not have done so if she had actually taken in a lodger. For she had never been forbidden to do this; and after her children had left home she had previously had a lodger for nine years. This was under the same landlord who was now trying to get her out; and he had made no objection at all.

Because the case against her was practically non-existent, the solicitor included in his letter an offer of what he called suitable alternative accommodation – not as one might expect at another address, but in the same house. He informed the old lady that she had 'accommodation in excess of her requirements' and could have a smaller tenancy: the three rooms upstairs or the three rooms downstairs, whichever she preferred. She was assured that the rent would be most reasonable, but the amount was not stated nor was she even assured that her new tenancy would still be protected.

The old lady, who suffered from high blood pressure, became extremely agitated. She agreed that six rooms were too many for one person, even though they were all extremely small. But she felt she could not sleep on the ground floor – it was too airless; yet if she took the floor upstairs she would have no kitchen. Terrified that she would have to get out if she did not accept, she sent her married daughter to ask advice.

A letter was written to the landlord's solicitor, not mentioning this offer, but simply asking why the notice to quit had been sent on the sole evidence of an advertisement.

A longish silence followed during which the old lady repeatedly had to be assured that from the legal point of view she had nothing at all to fear. The landlord's solicitor, however, did not so easily give up trying. He wrote to inquire if the old lady had really understood the offer made to her.

The solicitor was then politely informed, in so many words, that the old lady understood the offer only too well, and that she realized that her landlord's purpose (as his solicitor later admitted) was to put new tenants – over whom she would have no control – into that part of the very small house which she was being pressed, after nearly fifty years, to give up. He was told that she was too old and ill to share the house with strangers and that her legal advisers felt that it was quite unreasonable to expect her to do so, especially since she would have to share the kitchen. She would also have to share the outdoor w.c. and to reach it either she would have to go through the new tenants' rooms, or they would have to go through hers. But this fact was kept in reserve.

By this time, five months of guerrilla warfare had passed and six letters had been written by the landlord's solicitor. His seventh suggested that total victory had been won: his clients would take no further action on the notice to quit and the old lady would be 'allowed' to occupy the house as before. But one question had all the time remained unanswered.

As the landlord (a property company) had held that the old lady had more living space than she needed, he had been asked, reasonably enough, if she might have permission to sub-let which would, of course, also cover the taking in of a lodger. She did not really need this permission. As she had never been forbidden to sub-let, she would have been in her rights to go ahead without asking. This, indeed, had made the landlord's original attack on her even more monstrous than she had then realized. But what had followed had naturally made her much too frightened to take in a lodger without permission – and in writing.

The solicitor said he would ask for his client's instructions on this point. Whether he himself had pointed out to his client that, in fact, the old lady's request could not be refused is not known. Then, after another long pause, came the most extraordinary development of all.

The landlord wrote saying that if his tenant had enough space to take in lodgers (she had never asked for more than one) she must surely be able to live on one floor herself and to let the other to the lodgers.

That might not have looked like a trap to anyone unacquainted with the ways of wicked landlords, but a trap it most certainly was. For if the old lady had agreed to let her lodger have a separate floor, her whole case against dividing the house would have collapsed.

At the time of writing the landlord has been asked why he is taking such an interest in the way his tenant proposes to accommodate a lodger, since it would appear that she possesses a perfect right to share her rooms as she thinks best. The reply, if there is one, should be interesting. It should perhaps be added that much of this battle was fought without the knowledge of the old lady herself. In her condition anything but good news might have killed her.

During the final stages of this campaign a very significant advertisement, relating to quite another case, appeared in the *London Property Letter* (a newsletter circulated chiefly to property owners) and was quoted in the *Guardian* of 29 October 1963:

Can anyone provide us with alternative accommodation for our statutory tenant at Twickenham, a single lady occupying three rooms. £500 for a quick practical solution.

On this the *Guardian* aptly commented:

Does the single lady of Twickenham know what she is worth? If she is proving so expensive to her landlord it may be that she likes her home, even cherishes it, and perhaps has spent money on it. At least she knows something of her rights. . . .

Notice to Quit

Without Warning or Reason. Sometimes a notice to quit is sent to a protected tenant not only without the usual warning letter but without any stated grounds for sending it. This, too, is quite lawful but it is sometimes used as a means of intimidation. Of course grounds have to be given to a court in any claim for possession of a rent-controlled house, and of course the tenant gets a copy and can then enter a defence if he has one. But naturally he will not know this. The absence of any warning throws him into a panic; and he may start packing up because he feels that, if the all-powerful landlord is determined to get him out, his chances of being able to resist will be nil.

This happened in the case of a widower who had been the tenant of a rent-controlled house for over twenty years. But the landlord's agent was challenged and very quickly withdrew the notice saying that it had been sent in error. This was a little hard to believe because the agent had a notoriously bad name and was at the same time extremely efficient.

False Accusation of Rent Arrears. In worse cases the landlord asks for the rent book to be returned to him 'for audit' and then either sends a new book with rent arrears entered in it, or sends back the old one with the receipts crossed out or some pages removed and, again, arrears entered in it although nothing is owed. As this is a punishable offence, landlords usually withdraw such allegations the moment they realize that their very sharp practice has been detected.

Although it is sometimes difficult to be sure that what looks like a trick really is one, there are certain cases where trickery stares one in the face.

Deceptive Offers

Sometimes a protected tenant gets a very surprising and apparently free offer to move into better and bigger rooms but still at the same low rent. This is not an 'alternative' offer and no notice to quit comes with it. So it can easily seem to the tenant that the landlord is acting out of the kindness of his heart.

The usual purpose, of course, is to get two decontrolled tenancies: the one vacated and the one offered. Notice to quit from the new address often follows within a couple of weeks.

It did so in the case of two elderly spinster sisters who afterwards became homeless and had to go into an institution. Like many elderly people they were sitting targets for this sort of trick. And their landlord had expressly made himself charming to them beforehand, telling them that he felt that old people have a raw deal in this country and that it gave him great pleasure to be able to do something to help them.

Exchanges

People in the social services are often deceived by this sort of approach too. And they are sometimes delighted by the fact that a landlord seems surprisingly cooperative about a proposed exchange of rent-controlled tenancies between one of their clients or patients who desperately wants to move, and another protected tenant who is just as eager.

Under the law, controlled tenancies can be exchanged or assigned with the landlord's consent. But if it is pointed out to him that both tenancies must afterwards remain controlled, his consent – which of course ought to be (but seldom is) in the form of a properly drawn up and stamped agreement – is usually very quickly withdrawn. The reason for this is that he has been counting on the tenants' ignorance and has been hoping to use the exchange as a means of charging a higher rent. Naturally he is not going to bother about an arrangement which will give him no advantage – still less about one which could prove a positive disadvantage.

It could be that his tenant is old and lives alone and has been forbidden to sub-let, or does not want to. Obviously the prospect of getting vacant possession will be brighter the older the tenant is. No business-like landlord, therefore, is going to ruin his chances by letting that tenant exchange with a young family which badly needs the extra space, unless he can afterwards get them out when it suits him, or unless he happens to be of saintly and self-denying character.

Smoking Out

The Rachman property scandals exposed a really horrifying trick which the public took to be a new one but which, unhappily, is not: that of smoking out protected tenants. This is done by putting into the same house other tenants who are encouraged by the landlord to make as much noise, dirt, and unpleasantness as possible. Usually these planted tenants are coloured immigrants, calculated to inspire extra terror by their very blackness. And the landlord uses them merely as pawns. For after they have served his purpose he can clear the board of them with the greatest ease.

Often, though, the mere threat of this treatment is quite enough for the tenant – who gets out and goes heaven knows where with all possible speed. Or a proposal to let half the house to coloured people, with no suggestion that they will cause any disturbance, will do the trick – so great and easily exploitable are ignorance and prejudice.

Some agents quite openly and shamelessly tell intending house-buyers (and I mean private individuals buying for their own use) that they can undertake to smoke protected tenants out for them in this way if they are set on buying with vacant possession. Alternatively they may suggest that the buyer could do this for himself after the contract is signed. One or two old-established and reputable firms in some of the best parts of London have been known to suggest this; and without even first finding out whether or not the client is totally opposed to the exploitation of coloured people on the one hand, and to all forms of intimidation towards tenants on the other.

Counter-Action. A person to whom such a suggestion is made in the privacy of an agent's office cannot do much about it unless he has a witness, or does not fear an action for slander. What can put a stop to it is for a third party to ring up the agent and inquire politely if this is the agent's usual practice in negotiating such sales. A Citizens' Advice Bureau or an information office has an excellent reason for doing this on its own account because it will have a list of all the reputable agents in its area, which it will naturally amend as necessary.

On the other hand, a tenant in the process of being smoked out or threatened with this fate, as a private individual, has much more freedom to act than his advisers are likely to possess. And there is nothing at all to prevent him from letting the agent or landlord know that he proposes to get publicity for his case, preferably via television. He can also mention that he is going to report to his M.P. and his local council. This sort of action is of course only feasible for people of considerable courage. But one man, recently threatened in this way, simply told the landlord that it would not worry him to have coloured people in the house as he had always got on excellently with them at work.

Offers of Money

Another well-known and, superficially, quite unobjectionable method of getting a protected tenant out is to offer him enough money to put a deposit on a house, or even enough to buy one outright. As long as he is not coerced, and knows about all the difficulties and extra expenses that buying a house entails, and has consulted a solicitor, there is nothing to worry about. What may appear to be bribery is really a business transaction with mutual advantages. And for the tenant, it may be the chance of a lifetime.

But legal advice is essential to make sure that the offer is a fair one. In the case of an offer of money for a deposit, the tenant may find out too late that he cannot get a mortgage because of his age or his earnings; and for a woman the mortgage difficulty will be far more severe. Perhaps, too, the tenant will not have much idea about house prices. He may find that the sum offered will not buy anything in a decent condition – except perhaps in the depths of the country where he will probably find himself unemployed.

It is a terrible temptation to badly off people to accept any sum to get out of their homes if that has always been their hitherto hopeless ambition; and almost any sum can look like big money to them. Besides, they will probably have not the slightest idea of the profit that the landlord stands to get from the deal.

Above all, an offer of, say £100 or less should be regarded with extreme suspicion, especially if the landlord says he has a friend who for that amount will find the tenant another and much better flat. For the landlord's friend, or his flats, or both, may turn out not to exist. And £100 would now barely be enough for key money on a flat in the worst neighbourhoods (in London at any rate). Worst of all, as the law stands now the tenancy would be decontrolled.

In other cases the landlord may offer a small sum of money for the tenant to move into another of his own properties. The money may seem to the tenant adequate compensation for giving up his protective rights. But a solicitor would be sure to tell him that he should not move at all unless he is offered a lease of at least ten years, and preferably fifteen, on his new home – always provided, of course, that the solicitor is not also acting for the landlord. But only a disreputable solicitor would act for a tenant where his and his landlord's interests conflicted in this way; and he would be liable to disciplinary action by the Law Society.

Danger Through Take-overs

When the word goes round that a new landlord has taken over a row of houses, or a block of flats, or a tenement, or even a whole street – that is a time to look out for trickery. For the object of buying is often to sell again almost immediately – after having displaced the maximum number of protected tenants in the interval, which will greatly increase the value of the property for reselling.

In a recent case one property company sold a row of dingy rent-controlled houses to another company. An agent was then sent to call on the protected tenants, all of whom were elderly people. He appeared without warning on a Sunday afternoon and encouraged them to talk about their domestic affairs. All he said at the time was that in the future the rent would not be collected weekly but must be posted monthly to an address in the country.

On this visit, however, the agent must have noted which of the old people were not living alone. For within a week they received frightening solicitors' letters accusing them of sub-letting without permission and commanding them to get rid of their sub-tenants forthwith or legal proceedings would be taken.

One of these elderly tenants had some relatives living with her. She had taken in her niece and brother-in-law after his wife had died; and for eighteen years they had been living as one family, sharing meals and expenses. In other words there was no sub-tenancy at all. Next door there were certainly some sub-tenants living in the upper half of the house. But they were the last of an unbroken series, and permission to sub-let had been granted. In fact it was first granted, with advice on how much to charge, during the war.

This landlord's very typical technique was to fire first and ask questions afterwards. He got some unexpected answers and was eventually forced to retreat. But the tenants got little pleasure from their victory: they paid for it not only in anxiety but in actual illness.

Before long the landlord returned to the attack. He sent his agent to a third house where an old couple were taking a small rent from their married daughter. The daughter had lived in the house since she was born. The agent suggested that she might like to be a tenant rather than a sub-tenant as her position would, he made out, be safer when the property was resold. This of course was quite untrue but she did not know it. As she was still to pay the same very low rent as she had paid to her mother, she naturally saw no reason to be suspicious, and she therefore accepted a new rent book. What was the object of this exercise? Obviously to get decontrol of her half of the house by giving her a new tenancy. But this was a try-on if ever there was one. For her parents had the tenancy of the whole house and the landlord had no power whatsoever to grant a separate tenancy in it. When challenged, he hastily withdrew.

Other Manoeuvres for Profit

Anyone not acquainted with the ways of property companies might think this sort of game hardly worth the candle. But when selling parcels of assorted houses and tenants there is a great advantage in being able to advertise as many decontrolled items as possible, even if the new landlord is going to find that they are duds on which he cannot cash in; for this is a cut-throat game all round, and there is no loyalty among landlords. This is why one often finds tenants who have merely been manoeuvred into dubious positions, well camouflaged by deceptively low rents. Another advantage to the seller is that by these manoeuvres, conducted by agents, he avoids having to find, and pay, a solicitor unscrupulous enough to carry out his instructions.

For these reasons an unnaturally low rent entered in a newly bestowed rent book should always be suspect. And there is an additional and quite different reason for saying this, a reason which concerns a death in the family.

After a Death

The 1957 Rent Act preserved the right – in certain circumstances – to inherit security of tenure, or, to be more exact, the right to retain possession of a controlled house. When a protected tenant dies any member of his family who has been living with him for the last six months or more can remain in possession as a 'statutory tenant' – a widow always having priority. But that right cannot be passed on again to a third relative. This is what is meant by the mystifying phrase 'The rent book can only pass once'. Often, however, it does not pass at all because the person to whom it should go is not aware of his rights and is most unlikely to hear of them from the landlord.

Here is a typical story told me by a London taxi-driver. He had started by saying that he was lucky in having his own house. By that he did not mean that he owned it but that he had the tenancy of the whole of it. It had been in a very bad state when he took it over and he was enjoying doing it up. 'Of course,' he said, 'we were very fortunate. A couple of years ago my wife and I gave up a nice flat to go and look after her father. He only had his pension and was quite on his own. His wife had died some time back. Of course we were very upset to lose him – he died just recently. And we were scared that if the landlord let us have the house he'd charge us a rent we couldn't afford. You see, the wife's father had only been paying 30s. and we couldn't hope for that to continue. But the landlord was very fair about it, very fair indeed. He only put the rent up 50 per cent.' Sometimes one is almost sorry to disillusion people about the fairness of their landlords. But the taxi-driver's wife clearly needed a solicitor. Quite apart from the question of rent, the right to inherit security of tenure is nowadays far too precious to lose by default.

Joint Tenancies

Some rent-controlled tenancies were originally granted in the joint names of husbands and wives. Trouble can arise after a husband or wife dies and the widow or widower becomes the sole tenant, because the landlord may claim that in this process the rent book has already 'passed'. As a claim of this sort would not succeed in court, landlords sometimes try to bluff those concerned into believing that it would. This was done in the recent case of a family with six children who had lived with the children's paternal grandparents for many years as part of their household. On the death of the grandmother (the grandfather had died long before) the landlord's agent issued a new rent book with 'decontrolled' printed on it and at a rent £3 a week higher than was chargeable. The children's father was told – though not in writing – that he must either accept this or get out as his status was simply that of a trespasser. He would have accepted this ultimatum and, as he could not afford the rent, might have become homeless if he had not been a member of a tenants' association. His case is now being handled by a solicitor.

Private Contracts

There are several other long-term stratagems through which landlords can gain possession of rent-controlled houses. They involve privately arranged contracts of various kinds between landlords and sitting tenants. The tenant is induced to agree to whatever is proposed on the ground that he stands to gain much greater security than the Rent Acts can give him. And it is often pointed out that his existing protection is likely to be removed altogether by a Conservative government. After the contract has been signed the tenant can be quite easily tricked into some very small breach which allows the landlord to dispose of him. As some of these practices have not been publicized it would not be in the interests of tenants to go into details here. Some property companies have told their shareholders publicly that they can expect increased profits on a considerable scale by this means. The victims are often old people.

Refusing Rent

What does it mean when a tenant says that his landlord is refusing to take his rent? It could mean, quite simply, that a four weeks' notice to quit has expired and that the landlord is protecting himself from any claim to have granted a new tenancy (although he has other means of doing so). But where no notice to quit has been served it could, and sometimes does, mean that the landlord is going to try to claim that the tenant has refused or failed to pay his rent; in fact this is not an uncommon form of intimidation. The best way of putting a stop to it is to advise the tenant to offer the rent in the presence of a witness and to tell the landlord that he has been advised to do this. But if his rent is still refused he should open a post office savings account and pay it in week by week. If his case comes to court and he produces his paying-in book, the judge will recognize this as evidence of his good faith. It is a long-established means of defence.

But the surprising thing about this form of intimidation is the length of time that some landlords will persist in inflicting it, in the hope of wearing the tenant down. In one current case I know of it has already gone on for two years.

One might think that a landlord would not be prepared to go without his rent for nearly as long as that; but if it is a very low controlled rent (perhaps because he has failed to carry out repairs) the loss will matter very little if in the end he can get decontrol or vacant possession. Obviously it is always the most honest and respectable tenants who suffer most under this pressure because it worries them severely not to be paying their way. Some have been reduced to nervous wrecks. They never know when the landlord may suddenly demand the whole amount or when a summons may arrive.

*

These few examples should be enough to show how many forms trickery and intimidation can take and how sordid the whole business is.

What characterizes the victims is that none of them are bad tenants, or they could be disposed of by lawful means. Their crime is that they are obstacles to great potential profit, infuriating flies in the landlord's ointment.

But of course there are other cases where the rights of landlords and tenants clash, and where it is impossible even for experienced solicitors to guess which of them will win if the case goes to court.

With all these complications it is not always possible, let alone easy, to distinguish what is trickery from what is not; and where there is any doubt the landlord should be given the benefit of it. What is most important is to be able to recognize the danger signs and to see that the tenant gets legal advice – and quickly, or he may find himself out on his neck. If he becomes homeless he may be separated from his wife and children, and the children may eventually have to be taken into public care where they could be separated even from each other. And if the tenant is old he may find himself in an institution and never again have a home to call his own.

This chapter has been chiefly concerned with the techniques of 'de-statting' as practised on protected tenants; and with the foiling of these manoeuvres, which demands knowledge of the tenant's rights. The next chapter deals with dangers to tenants and to sub-tenants, protected and unprotected, and does so in the form of a list, for two special reasons:

1. A tenant can quickly run through a list and see at once if any of the risks apply to him now, or might do so in the future.
2. There are certain dangers about which tenants ought to be warned but – in their own best interests – only by the briefest mention. The purpose of certain moves by landlords can more safely be explained to them in private.

3 What Are the Danger Signs?

Nowadays, any communication from a landlord – however harmless it may look – can turn out to be an unexploded bomb. So it is very important to know what signs of possible danger to look for.

There are special dangers which apply to tenants (who pay their rent direct to the landlord), and others for sub-tenants (who do not). There are also general dangers.

TENANTS

A tenant who gets a letter or message from his landlord (or from his landlord's solicitor, or agent, or rent collector) should not answer it before getting expert advice if there is any kind of accusation, proposal, request, or statement about a change of circumstances in it.

Typical Accusations

Tenants may be accused, among other things, of:
1 sub-letting, or taking in lodgers or relatives without permission;
2 sub-letting at an 'excessive rent';
3 sub-letting a bigger part of the house than was agreed with the landlord;
4 damaging the house or not keeping it clean;
5 overcrowding the house;
6 using the house for business, or for immoral purposes;
7 disturbing other tenants;
8 being in arrears of rent;
9 having 'broken the terms of the tenancy'.

Typical Proposals

A tenant may be asked if he would like:

1 to have fewer rooms at a reasonable or reduced rent in the house in which he already lives;
2 to take over a part of the house which has been vacated, in addition to the part in which he lives;
3 to take over the tenancy of the whole house;
4 to move to another floor;
5 to move to another address (with or without an offer of money);
6 to buy his landlord's furniture, or to sell his own furniture to the landlord;
7 to sign a tenancy agreement or any other document;
8 to pay for repairs in exchange for the withdrawal of a notice to quit;
9 to buy the house by instalments.

Typical Statements

A tenant may be told that:

1 he has 'accommodation in excess of his requirements', i.e. more rooms than he needs;
2 his home has become decontrolled;
3 the rateable value of his home is now above the control limit;
4 would-be tenants with orders to view will be calling to look over the house;
5 part of the house will be, or has been, re-let to coloured tenants;
6 the house is being sold privately or to the local authority;
7 vacant possession of the house will be required by its new owner;
8 the house is needed by the landlord for himself or his parents or grown-up children;
9 the house is needed for an employee of the landlord;
10 the house is needed by the local authority for clearance;
11 the local authority requires that the number of people in the house shall be reduced and/or that the house must be repaired or improved;

12 the tenancy has come to an end and cannot be renewed.

Typical Requests

Tenants may be asked:
1 to send the landlord a list of everyone living in the house;
2 to get rid of sub-tenants, lodgers, or relatives;
3 to return rent books to the landlord or collector.

No tenant or sub-tenant need fear that legal advice from a solicitor will cost him more than he can afford (see Chapter 1).

Offers of Extra Accommodation

Tenants (including sub-tenants who have become tenants, see below) should get legal advice before taking over any extra accommodation in a house. They may be entitled to take this over at a controlled rent especially if the accommodation consists only of an extra room or two. But if it consists of living space formerly occupied by another tenant, with a kitchen or scullery, the tenant who takes it over may be *entitled to have a separate rent book* for it, in addition to the one he already holds for the part of the house in which he has been living.

If he is given this new rent book and is advised that he now has two tenancies (one rent-controlled and one decontrolled) he should be very careful not to move into the decontrolled part of the house, leaving the rent-controlled part vacant – even if that part is upstairs and the roof leaks. He could find himself evicted.

In fact it is dangerous for tenants of privately owned property to make any move at all or to accept, or make, any proposal without finding out what the consequences could be.

SUB-TENANTS

A sub-tenant pays his rent only to a tenant – who is very often a relative – not to the owner of the house. He usually has his own means of cooking, and he should have a rent book. But if he shares rooms with the tenant, or if his rent includes a sizeable charge for meals, he may count in law as a lodger. He should get advice about this, because a lodger is not entitled to four weeks' notice to quit as a sub-tenant is, and has no security of tenure.

A sub-tenant can only be given notice to quit or have his rent raised (if the law allows this) by the tenant. The tenant is his landlord-in-law and is known as the sub-landlord. The owner of the house is known as the head landlord.

When the Tenant Leaves or Dies

As long as the tenant pays rent for the house, lives in it, and is not breaking any rule or agreement by sub-letting, the sub-tenant is in no danger from the owner of the house or his agents.

But if the tenant leaves to live somewhere else, or is evicted, or dies, the sub-tenant should immediately get advice about how he stands. (So, too, should any member of the tenant's family who, before his death, had been living with him for the last six months.)

A Right to Stay On. A sub-tenant may find that after the tenant has gone he has a right to stay on. If so he need not worry if his rent is not collected for a time. He will probably be told later to pay it to the owner or landlord. He will then become a tenant. If this happens, the dangers which apply to tenants (see page 52) will apply to him.

On the other hand, he could be told to pay his rent to a new tenant who has taken over the whole house. If so, he would remain a sub-tenant.

Insecurity

The sub-tenant may find, when he gets advice, that after the tenant has gone his position is not as safe as he had hoped. Even if the landlord is accepting his rent (so making him a tenant) that can still be so. It will depend on whether or not his sub-tenancy was decontrolled.

He could find that he is in danger of having his rent raised at some future date or of getting four weeks' notice to quit whether or not he is guilty of any offence.

GENERAL DANGERS
Notices to Quit
A notice to quit should never be taken lying down, even if it is

sent by a solicitor. It may be based on an offence which can be disproved; it could easily be faulty; it could be sent just as a formality, for instance when a long lease is coming to an end and a new one will be offered; or it could be nothing but bluff.

If a notice to quit is sent with an offer of 'alternative accommodation' it should certainly not be assumed that this offer must be accepted. It must be a reasonable offer from the tenant's point of view. But even if he likes the sound of it, he must get legal advice before accepting, otherwise he could lose his security.

Unwritten Messages and Private Interviews

If a tenant is simply told by the rent collector that his rent is going up, or that there is going to be some other unpleasant change, he should beware. It may not have struck him that because his landlord has chosen this method of getting in touch with him – rather than writing – he may be up to tricks.

Even more to be feared is an invitation from the landlord or his agent for the tenant to come to the office for a private interview. Of course there need not necessarily be anything in the least sinister about this, but it could be a spider-and-fly move.

When tenants have accepted invitations of this kind they have sometimes found themselves falsely accused afterwards of having admitted to some kind of tenancy offence. Or they have been persuaded to sign agreements that they did not understand. Sometimes a tenant is told that, for reasons which are quite beyond him, he no longer has any right to stay on in his home but that the landlord has kindly decided to grant him a new tenancy. The rent, he may be told, will be a little more than it used to be but not much more, certainly not more than he can afford. A proposal of this kind, made in private, should never be accepted on the spot. It could easily mean that, in fact, the tenant has a right to stay on and at his old rent. A tenant should never go alone to an interview of this kind and should get advice before it and also immediately after it, while he still remembers exactly what was said.

Pressing Offers to Buy

A landlord who wants to get rid of his property at almost any price and in a hurry – perhaps because he is faced with a local authority repair order – may propose that the tenant should buy it and will often do this by letter and in terms suggesting that the tenant has no other choice if he wants to stay on. This, of course, is not so if his tenancy is rent-controlled.

A Special Danger. A tenant can be asked if he would like to buy the house simply by continuing to pay a weekly sum which may be no more, or not much more, than his present rent. In such cases the landlord rarely provides any form of contract, and usually forbids the tenant to consult any solicitor but his own – if he has one.

These proposals are highly dangerous. At any time the landlord can, if it suits him, deny that there has been any arrangement to sell. He is likely to do this after he has obliged the tenant to pay for repairs. Or he may simply raise the amount of the instalments or make the tenant go on paying them after the purchase price has been reached, as 'interest'. Even when the tenant has finished paying he can be – and many tenants have been – denied the deeds of the house.

Dangers of Official Visits

1. *National Assistance*. A tenant who is unable to work may have to apply for national assistance. If his tenancy is unprotected, and if his landlord lives in the house and has put a ban on officials coming to it, he should ask the National Assistance Board if it can possibly arrange to assist him without first making the usual visit to his home. If this is refused, as it will be if he is unable to work for more than a week or two, he should try to arrange the visit when the landlord is out. Otherwise notice to quit may follow.

Tenants may also find that they cannot be granted national assistance unless they can show a rent book, yet it may be unsafe to ask the landlord for one. This should be explained to the

National Assistance Board with, if necessary, the help of a Citizens' Advice Bureau.

2. *Public Health.* There will be an even greater danger if the tenant calls in a sanitary, or public health, inspector to look at a leaking roof or some other defect, because the landlord may be required to repair them.

3. *Rent Tribunals.* Application to a rent tribunal is similarly dangerous because this, too, involves an official visit to the house and because the tribunal may afterwards reduce the rent.

NOTE *None of the above dangers apply to people with rent-controlled tenancies because they have security of tenure. Also, there is no danger in applying to a Citizens' Advice Bureau or an information office because this does not involve a home visit.* However it is best not to tell the landlord that any kind of outside help is being sought.

Tenancy Agreements

Tenancy agreements often take the form of a printed document on which the landlord enters his terms and which the tenant is simply asked to sign. See also pages 64 and 88.

These documents are, in one sense, rather like the agreement forms used for hire purchase: nearly all the conditions protect the owner, and very few indeed the hirer or, in this case, the tenant. Also, the language used is just as hard to understand.

A would-be tenant may be strongly tempted to sign on the dotted line without reading the conditions, especially if he is told that if he does not sign at once the flat he wants will go to someone else.

This is just the sort of situation in which he is likely to be tricked. Here is an extreme example.

A West Indian, who could not read and who could barely write his name, was so desperate to get a home for his family that in the privacy of an agent's office he signed a proposal that for one year he should pay rent at £16 a week. This was for a slum house with eight rooms, two of which were in a basement and were much too damp to use. At the end of the year the agent invited this very valuable tenant to his office and said he would be pleased to renew the agreement on exactly the same terms, but this time for three years. Not long afterwards the tenant asked a public health inspector to look at the leaking roof. Furious at being required to repair it, the agent told the tenant he would get him out. This did not at first worry the tenant because he thought he had security for three years. But when his agreement was looked at, it was found to be quite different from the one he had been given before, and that among its many conditions was one forbidding him to sub-let. The agent had known that the tenant could not read and that he would have to sub-let to pay the rent, because he earned only £11 a week. But in the eyes of the law he had broken his agreement, and he was therefore in danger of losing his home.

There were, however, two possible ways of protecting him. At one stage water from a burst pipe had made three of the rooms uninhabitable and, because of this, the agent had offered to take £13 a week instead of £16 until the pipe was repaired. Unknown to the tenant, he had then unlawfully entered £3 a week as arrears from that date onwards. Also, the agreement had not been stamped and that meant that no court could look at it.

Dangers of Signing Agreements Without Proper Inspection of Premises. Some would-be tenants have been persuaded to sign agreements without even seeing the flats or rooms offered; or they have been hustled round them, often at night, without a proper chance of finding out whether new wall paper is hiding damp patches or whether there will be enough space to squeeze in the children's beds.

One man forgot to look for gas and electric points. The agent assured him that there were points in both the rooms, but this was quite untrue. The rooms, behind a shop, had been used for storage; so the tenant's wife found herself with no means of cooking.

It also frequently happens that people who have been pressed into signing agreements, or into paying key money or rent in advance, have afterwards found that there was no place to hang out washing, or for parking a pram, or even for emptying their rubbish.

Assigning. If the landlord agrees, a tenant can free himself from a tenancy agreement by assigning it to someone else. But it is not always easy to find just the right person. And if the tenant who takes over later fails to pay his rent, the original tenant can be held responsible.

A rent-controlled tenancy can also be assigned, or exchanged. In all these cases the landlord's agreement *must*, for safety, be in writing.

Importance of Solicitor Vetting Agreement. A good reason for having an agreement vetted by a solicitor is that it may have a genuine but very important mistake in it. Recently an agreement was entered by an agent as being binding for three weeks instead of three years.

Importance of Keeping a Copy of an Agreement. Sometimes a landlord will keep an agreement which the tenant has signed, but refuse to give him a copy. This can be very awkward for a tenant if he is later commanded to carry out repairs or to pay more rent. But the landlord will be in an awkward position if he tries to sue for breach of contract.

Notice of Leaving. Where there is no agreement about the length of a tenancy, the tenant is bound by law to give the landlord four weeks' notice of leaving. If he does not, the landlord can claim four weeks' rent.

This can be very awkward if the tenant gets a chance of better and cheaper private accommodation which he must take at once and on which he has to pay rent in advance. It can be almost as awkward if he suddenly gets an offer of a council flat after years of waiting because these offers have to be accepted within a few days. Few tenants can possibly afford to pay two rents concurrently.

Most landlords can re-let at almost a moment's notice and therefore stand to get the benefit of two rents. They are usually willing, therefore, either to waive what is owed or to accept it in instalments. But there could be hardship to a small-scale landlord in a place where immediate re-letting is not easy.

Leases

If property is to be let for years rather than months, a lease – which is a legal deed – is more often used than the less formal tenancy agreement.

A lease drawn up by the landlord's solicitor should on no account whatever be signed – no matter how great the landlord's pressure – without the advice of an independent solicitor: the risks, otherwise, are tremendous. And they are even greater for anyone invited to buy, or even to accept as a gift, a lease due to expire in a few years. See also page 70.

Estate Agents

Membership of the Royal Institution of Chartered Surveyors, the Chartered Auctioneers' and Estate Agents' Institute, or the Incorporated Society of Auctioneers and Landed Property Agents is some guarantee of honesty because offences can be reported to them. But it is no absolute guarantee because alleged offences are very difficult to prove in the absence of witnesses, receipts, or written statements.

None of the agents mentioned in this book were members of any of these societies.

Reputation counts for more than anything else. The size of the firm counts for nothing. Honest estate agents suffer badly from the fact that so many entirely disreputable people, often quite unqualified, now operate in their field.

Apart from landlords and tenants, the people likely to know most about local estate agents are solicitors, surveyors, workers in information and advisory offices, public health inspectors, and rating officers.

Accommodation Agencies

The most reliable accommodation agencies supply intending tenants with a full list of charges and conditions and a guarantee that all the accommodation on their lists has been inspected by members of their staff and has not been found to be sub-standard or worse. Usually what the tenant has to pay to the agency is the amount of one week's rent, apart, of course, from any extra charges made by the landlord.

The chief risk is from agencies which demand deposits on accommodation which either does not exist or cannot lawfully be let or which turns out to be uninhabitable. An agency which has no offices and operates through a postal box number, or which refuses to supply any written or printed terms, or which does not give the names of its directors on its handouts, is more than suspect.

Demolition Orders

When a local council tells a negligent landlord that it proposes to issue a demolition order on a house (one which is not due to come down with others as part of a clearance scheme but which has been condemned as unfit for human habitation) the landlord can ward this off by undertaking to carry out the repairs. If he does this the local authority is under no obligation to rehouse the tenant, temporarily or otherwise; and the tenant may have to stay on while the house is taken to pieces over his head, even if he is deprived of water, heating, lighting, and the means of cooking in the process. The landlord need not find him anywhere else to live (*if he does, he may use this as a means of getting decontrol*), but can maintain that he is unable to repair the house with the tenant in it.

Closing Orders

The issue of a closing order on a house does not mean that it will be shut up and the tenant rehoused. It means little more than that after the present tenant has left it must not be let again. Very often only the basement is 'closed' which does not mean that it is sealed off (often this is impossible anyway because the water supply is in it). Landlords who do not unlawfully let such basements often fail to reduce the controlled rent of the house although the closing of any part of it naturally reduces its rateable value.

Bailiffs

Information on landlord and tenant rights on this grim subject should be sought in private.

Repairs

So many dangers come under this heading that they have been given a chapter to themselves (Chapter 4, page 67).

Rates

Most weekly tenants pay rent inclusive of rates; those with controlled tenancies almost always do so. Their rent can therefore go up or down from year to year. Landlords rarely fail to put the rent up in respect of a rates increase, but they often fail to reduce it when they should; and the amounts they charge are often wrong.

Where rates have gone down, and rents with them, there is sometimes trouble if a new landlord takes over because he finds that the inclusive rents that he is able to charge are lower than those that were advertised. Some landlords try to make tenants pay at the former, and higher, inclusive rent and enter arrears if they refuse. This can soon be stopped by the local authority. So can attempts by landlords to make protected tenants pay double rates by charging them inclusive rents and sending them rate demands as well. But tenants of decontrolled property without agreements will run the risk of eviction if they contest overcharged rates.

In the Case of Untraceable Landlords. Where a landlord has de-camped and cannot be traced, which quite often happens, the tenants have to pay the rates (as well as Schedule A tax) direct to the local authority. Usually they are allowed to do this in in-stalments. Of course, the rates come to less than the rent, and sometimes tenants forget to save the difference. Then, a year or so later, the landlord reappears and claims the difference, re-fusing to take it in instalments.

Sub-letting and Taking Lodgers

A weekly tenant without an agreement who wants to sub-let can find himself in a very tricky position.

He has a right to sub-let unless he has been forbidden to do so, or has agreed not to do so without first asking the landlord's permission.

If he takes legal advice about this last point he is likely to be told (a) that the landlord cannot withhold his permission unreasonably and (b) that he, the tenant, will run risks if he does not get this permission in writing.

The result often is that the landlord refuses to put anything in writing so that the tenant has no proof of acceptance, and therefore does not dare to go ahead.

On the other hand, a tenant who has been forbidden to sub-let can still take a lodger (see page 40) – as long as he has not agreed to use the house for 'private dwelling' only.

What makes all this more complicated is that a tenant of rent-controlled property usually has no idea that he has agreed to anything at all. At the beginning of his tenancy he was simply given a rent book and told how much rent to pay. Perhaps there were some printed regulations inside the front cover but he was not asked to agree to them or to sign them. It can come as a great shock to find that they represent a contract and that part of it may forbid him to sub-let or to take in lodgers.

But, fortunately for him, the landlord's position may be almost as difficult. He probably did not provide the original rent book, and it may have been thrown away years ago. He may have little or nothing to go on if he wants to take legal proceedings against a tenant who is already sub-letting. And if he has been doing this for five years or more, it is going to be rather embarrassing for the landlord to tell a court that he did not know what was going on in his property for all that time.

Tenants of decontrolled property are usually forbidden to sub-let as a matter of course. If not, they may be advised that they have a right to sub-let but would be very rash to exercise it.

Paying the Rent

A new tenant ought to make certain whether he is to pay his rent to the landlord or to the agent, as the agent may not be entitled to take it. Very disreputable agents sometimes take rent but do not pass it on, or not all of it, to the landlord.

Landlords can make their own rules about how the rent is to be paid. Tenants may have to send it by post. Only those with security of tenure should risk deducting the cost of postal orders and stamps; and that applies also to standing on the right to refuse a proposal by the landlord to alter his original arrangement for payment.

Rent in Advance. Wicked landlords often refuse to acknowledge, at the end of a tenancy, that at the beginning of it they took rent in advance. They do their best to make the tenant pay twice.

However, if the landlord has failed to supply a rent book, he will have no proof that he took the rent in arrear; and he will be in a rather embarrassing position if the case goes to court.

Withholding Rent. It is always dangerous for a tenant to withhold his rent even if his roof is behaving like a colander and his bed is sinking through the floorboards. There have been cases where the withholding of rent has jolted the landlord into carrying out repairs to rent-controlled property. But the landlord's usual and natural reaction is to issue a notice to quit for arrears of rent.

In certain very special circumstances, which will be explained in Chapter 4, a tenant of rent-controlled property can reduce his rent, and there are circumstances in which no rent is due from him because he has overpaid it – which, unfortunately, is not at all the same thing as being overcharged.

Deposits, Key-money, Premiums, etc.

There can be great difficulty in reclaiming a deposit if the house or rooms on which it was paid are not taken, unless a receipt was given stating exactly what the payment represented.

Requests for any kind of receipt are always refused by the worst landlords, and the money has to be paid in cash.

If the rooms are taken, the tenant may find it impossible to get back his deposit when he leaves. In cases recently reported in Hampstead and St Pancras, tenants who asked for their deposits back found their doors padlocked, their belongings gone, or the gas pipes and electric wiring cut so that they were forced out. This treatment is not unusual elsewhere.

It is not illegal to demand a premium or a cash payment of any kind as a condition of granting a decontrolled or uncontrolled tenancy, for less than 21 years, furnished or unfurnished. It is still illegal to ask for any payment other than rent on a controlled tenancy.

For fixtures and fitting charges see under Furnished Accommodation, page 88.

Improvement Grants

If a landlord proposes to improve a house with the help of a grant the tenant should not agree without taking advice on increase of rent which will follow, or possible loss of living space, and on future security of tenure.

TENANTS WITH SPECIAL CIRCUMSTANCES

Tenants in special circumstances – for instance living in farmhouses or tied cottages, or whose tenancy includes a shop or office – may not face any special immediate danger but ought to arm themselves with information about their position. There is a list of special circumstances on page 30.

*

This mixed bag of dangers and pitfalls, for quick checking and early warning, needs some apology because it is not, of course, anything like a full one. New dangers are constantly cropping up as landlords become more ingenious; and no comprehensive all-risks list exists, or ever has existed, for reference. On the other hand some of the worst risks demand chapters to themselves – and will now get them.

4 The Repairs Racket

In our unreasonably wet climate houses do not live very long unless they are solidly built and tenderly cared for. As we are imprisoned in our houses for so much of the year, their defects cannot be lightly disregarded. They sit heavily on the mind – and can eat slowly into it like woodworm.

The great mass of privately owned, rented housing was built, chiefly in terraces, eighty or more years ago. During the war, when these houses were in their middle age, those which escaped destruction or damage had practically no repairs done to them, and this continued for years afterwards. The clearance of unfit or diseased houses did not begin in earnest until nine years ago and has proceeded with painful slowness, so that now it is estimated that we need half a million new houses a year simply to keep pace with the housing 'death rate'. That estimate may sound exaggerated, but it could be too low. No one really knows how many houses are dying on their foundations, whether from old age or lack of proper attention. Information comes to local authorities chiefly from despairing tenants. But it is not disputed that literally millions of people, particularly in northern industrial cities, are living in houses which ought to have been swept into oblivion years ago. And all this has, of course, a very direct bearing on the thorny question of repairs and on who should be held responsible for them.

Before going into this, it needs to be said that the official term 'unfit for human habitation' now varies so widely in application from one place to another that it no longer has any definite meaning. In towns where there is no great shortage, houses in quite good health get this label because it is no great problem for those condemned to be replaced. But in cities with massive waiting lists, hovels in a state of decomposition have to be left uncondemned for years – and so do underground basements better fitted to grow mushrooms than children – because there is no spare accommodation in which to transplant the tenants – a situation which can greatly benefit private landlords.

In one of the worst cases I ever came across, part of the roof of a small terrace house had been open to the sky for years and dampness had ruined every room. Fungus sprouted from the walls and mildew coated everything in the cupboards. The tenant, aged seventy-five, who still had to pay rent, was confined to one room on the ground floor which was frequently flooded. Yet from the time her timid complaints were reinforced by those of her advisers it took another five years before a demolition order was issued.

More recently, in October 1963, a demolition order was served on a London house where a certificate of disrepair had been in force for years, and where the upper floor had been uninhabitable (except by birds) for just as long. What finally induced the borough council to take action was that it had been found impossible – because of the decaying fabric of the house – to keep rats out of it. They were big sewer rats and had become so bold that they were taking food off the kitchen table and dragging away the children's clothes to line their nests.

This house was not due to come down as part of a clearance scheme for at least another ten years – the other, not until after the year 2,000.

These are extreme examples; but at least they show what disrepair and unfitness can nowadays mean in the capital city, and under what conditions rent still has to be paid. In the rat-ridden house, owned by a property company, the upper floor was decontrolled and for a time fetched £2 10s. a week. On the ground floor the tenants were paying £1 3s. per week which, over the last two and a half years, represented an overcharge on the controlled rent of more than £70. In the flooded house where the old tenant lived, the rent of nearly £1 per week had for years been paid to the landlord by the public, through the National Assistance Board. It had covered the purchase price of the house many years ago.

REPAIR OBLIGATIONS FOR TENANTS WITH LEASES

To be obliged to repair someone else's house is always bitter, as anyone who has ever been a tenant with a repairing lease knows.

Leases can require the tenant to keep the house 'in good repair' – no matter how far less than good the state of repair was on taking over; or to be responsible for only internal repairs; or to take on all repairs inside and out, structural and otherwise – but that now applies only if the lease is for seven years or longer.

This last condition was made law only in October 1961; and tenants who have since then signed leases for less than seven years cannot be held responsible for structural or external repairs or for any that become necessary to the 'main installations' such as drains or water pipes. It was because so many landlords took advantage of decontrol to foist all repairs on their tenants, however incapable they were of paying for them, that this limit had to be made. A large crop of bankruptcies and slums would otherwise have resulted.

Almost needless to say, however, certain landlords have been getting round this restriction on their freedom by pressing tenants to sign repairing leases covering periods just over the limit. This has been reported as a growing practice in Manchester. It is one often used on unwary immigrants elsewhere. And another practice is to recoup what cannot now be charged for repairs by requiring lavish redecoration. For on this there are no restrictions.

Leases of 7–21 Years

A tenant who has signed a lease for any period of between seven and twenty-one years is now in a very unfair position. Even if he lives in a house with a very low rateable value, he has less protection under the law than he would if his lease were shorter or longer.

If the landlord wants possession of his home before the lease expires, this tenant can find himself quite unfairly accused of breach of contract on the repair clauses – which are frequently quite monstrously unfair in themselves – and can find himself obliged either to pay what is demanded or to fight the case in court. If this does not happen, he can of course be bled white with repair charges at the end of his time. Where there is no protection, repairing leases can be used by landlords to get their houses put in order at the tenant's expense without any obligation to keep him on.

Leases of Over 21 Years and Leasehold Property

The position of tenants with leases of over twenty-one years is now so immensely complicated that it is dangerous to say much about it. Because of efforts to provide some protection for long-term tenants of the lower rated houses (often elderly people in poor circumstances) the law has become a jungle of ifs and buts through which only solicitors can find their way. The protection, though valuable, is totally inadequate and does not prevent the charging of crippling sums for repairs. It is concerned more with limiting the grounds on which a landlord can claim possession, either during the lease or after it ends.

In houses above certain rateable value limits, the tenant has nothing but this contract to protect him, whether it was made with the owner of the freehold of his home or whether he bought his lease and pays rent to the ground landlord.

Tenants of leasehold property may have paid £50 for a lease or £50,000. They include some of the poorest and also the richest people in the country. Among the better-off, who can easily go elsewhere, it is a common practice to sell the tail end of a lease on an old house to avoid liability for dilapidations. And quite often nowadays the buyer is an unwary immigrant who, once he realizes his position, is obliged to sub-let at exorbitant rents and will make himself extremely unpopular in the process. But the less-well-off tenant will usually have no alternative but to stay on and foot the bill. However long a tenant of leasehold property lives in a house and repairs it he has no right to buy the freehold. If he gets the chance to buy it, the price asked may be, and often is, exorbitant.

Of course, landlords can find themselves cheated if, at the end of a lease, a tenant decamps to avoid liability for dilapidations.

But the system is open to much greater abuse by the landlord as dictator of terms. For instance, he can interfere with the tenant's liberty by *unreasonably* forbidding him to sub-let or to use part of the house as a surgery or for consulting rooms; and if legally obliged to keep him on as a statutory tenant can have the rent fixed by the courts after the tenant has paid for the initial repairs.

TENANTS AND SUB-TENANTS WITHOUT AGREEMENTS

Most tenants, however, have – for better or worse – no kind of agreement with their landlords except their rent books. Many, however, have no rent books. And more have rent books with no information, or with misleading information, in them.

These tenants fall into two groups: those with decontrolled tenancies and those whose tenancies are rent-controlled. Although tenants in both categories can, and often do, live in the same house, their positions about repairs are poles apart. Both, however, can be victims of the vilest trickery and intimidation.

Repairs in Decontrolled Accommodation

The man who with his family has taken a flat or rooms since 6 July 1957, and who has a grasping landlord, usually finds that he is utterly helpless about repairs. Because he has no agreement and no protection under the law, he has to risk retaliation if he dares to mention that the banisters have come away in his hand or the ceiling has come down on his head.

In a recent case, the father of five children, living in one room and a kitchen and paying £3 10s. a week for the privilege, asked a representative of the property company which owned the house to have the chimney stack attended to, as it was in a dangerous condition. The reply was that if this tenant wanted repairs, his rent must go up by £1 a week to pay for them. The man could not afford this. The repairs were not done, and a week or two later the chimney stack came crashing down, just missing the baby's pram.

In another case, a family with a new-born baby complained to the landlord that sewage from a blocked upstairs lavatory was seeping through their ceiling. They simply got notice to quit. And this made them homeless for the fourth time in less than two years.

In both these cases the tenants, although powerless themselves to compel their landlords to carry out necessary repairs, had a perfect right to ask at their town halls for this compulsion, under the Public Health Acts. But no one could safely advise them to do so, unless they were ready to take the risk of losing their homes.

There was also a risk, in both these cases, of endangering other tenants. For the houses were 'in multiple occupation', which means that they had been split up for letting, with several tenants – some single and some with families – each occupying one or two rooms. A request for repairs to the town hall always results in a visit from a public health inspector who, if he thinks fit, can require a landlord to 'reduce the number of persons' in such a house – and that, of course, means evicting the surplus. This is done under the Housing Act of 1961. (See also Chapter 7.)

A tenant in this wretched position can therefore be under pressure even from his fellow tenants not to ask for repairs. He is usually utterly bewildered when he discovers the extent of his helplessness to make his living conditions tolerable for his family. But the position of the man who does what he can about repairs himself can be almost as bad.

Doing Your Own Repairs. In poor districts of cities where thousands of small houses, and parts of houses, have become de-controlled – simply because they have been vacated since the Rent Act was passed, often because of a death – there is no need whatever for the landlord to smarten them up in order to re-let them at four or five times the rent they fetched when they were subject to control. By far the greatest demand for housing comes from families with low incomes who have always been used to poor conditions, who want to go on living near their work, and are desperately trying to escape from overcrowding or from living with relatives, or both.

Such young families will usually take any accommodation

offered, no matter how appalling its state of repair, to get themselves a little privacy, even if this means giving up a controlled rent and security of tenure. Those with the most initiative then set about plastering and papering and painting and, if they can afford it, put in new windows and doors and floorboards as well. The 'wicked landlord' is greatly delighted by this. The value of his property has been immeasurably increased without his having to lift a finger, and he calmly tells the tenant that it is now worth a higher rent. Perhaps the tenant cannot afford this but, even if he can, he will naturally resist. The landlord, however, has the last word – and it is eviction.

Sometimes a landlord whose decontrolled property has been vastly improved in this way will decide to sell and reap the profit. He may offer the house to the tenant. This happened to a man who had spent all his savings, £500, on turning a slum into something fit for his family to live in. As he could not pay the deposit asked as a condition of buying, he was turned out. The landlord offered him no compensation for his work, and when he consulted solicitors he found that he could claim none. This can only be done when the landlord has first agreed in detail and in writing to the work that the tenant proposes to undertake; and although this one had got his landlord's permission to do what he liked before starting, that was not at all the same thing as getting an agreement that the courts would recognize.

In a third and very recent case a young man who wanted to get married took part of the ground floor of a small house. It was in a poor district and was in a very bad condition. The landlord, who was buying the house on a mortgage, lived upstairs. He told the young man that he could do what he liked with the ground-floor rooms and need only pay £1 a week until he and his bride moved in. After that the rent vould be £2 10s.

The young man spent £150 on repairs, including the re-plastering of crumbling walls. After redecorating he installed an expensive sink unit and other furniture which he and his fiancée had laboured for years to buy. But the landlord, seeing how much more attractive the rooms now looked than his own, suddenly presented a quite unacceptable tenancy agreement at a higher rent, and did so on the very day the couple got married, at the same time calmly saying: 'Have a look at this and if there's anything you don't like in it, come back – and I'll show you the door.'

Even before the rooms were quite ready, this landlord had prepared the ground for making it impossible for the young couple to live in the same house with him on any terms. There was an old man living in one room on the ground floor who had once had a controlled tenancy of the whole of it – how he had lost all but one room is not known. The landlord, who felt sure that this old man had money tucked away, said he had frequently searched his room and looked under his mattress while he was out. He also boasted of what he had done to another tenant who had died in the house. He had found a purse attached to a belt round the old man's waist and had stolen it 'before the body was cold'.

The young man, who was once a boxer, does not trust himself to get within punching distance of this landlord. But after consulting two solicitors he is still without hope of compensation for repairing the house. What particularly riles him about all this is that the landlord is a working man like himself. He and others in the same position often remark that they can more easily accept being exploited if the landlord is a business man.

The fact that tenants of decontrolled property without agreements cannot be advised either to spend money on repairing their homes or to ask for repairs from the landlord or the local authority must result in a quite unnecessary increase in slums – and in bitterness.

Repairs in Rent-Controlled Property

There is a certain kind of trickery which deserves to be treated on its own because it has received practically no publicity and is of a special cruelty. It concerns, exclusively, tenants of rent-controlled property; and that means chiefly old people.

Only those who handled repair problems before and after 1957 know what a fantastic and unprecedented effect the Rent Act had on these so-called protected tenants. Under this Act the 1956 gross value of each house – or separately let part of it – was used as a basis for raising rents. A landlord who made himself responsible for repairs, inside and out, could charge double the gross value. If he chose to do the indoor decorations as well, he could charge a third more; and if he chose only to do the outside repairs he had to take a third less. In all three cases he could add the rates. But the Act also enabled the tenant to resist these increases if his reasonable requests for repairs were not met.

On paper this scheme looked fair. To the casual reader there was no reason why it should not work well for both landlord and tenant – each having something to gain. Besides, from the tenant's point of view, it seemed safe because he was protected against eviction. But that was reckoning without the wicked landlord with his eye to the main chance.

For instance, some landlords kicked off by bribing their tenants not to exercise their right to ask for repairs. Some promised, in exchange, not to raise the rent; others to raise it only a little. Tenants were told that if they did not sign away their rights they would be evicted. In a certain terrace of small houses only one tenant dared to resist, although all were assured that the threat of eviction was simply bluff.

In other cases tenants received similar threats if they dared to seek advice about their rights. Landlords' agents also made personal visits to many small houses and told tenants who had already sent in repair forms that they had fraudulently misrepresented the facts, and would pay for it when the police were informed.

On one such visit, to a pensioner aged seventy-eight, the agent was in the process of angrily maintaining that no repairs were needed when he fell through the floor. This story went the rounds gaily enough, but there were others that were tragic. An old woman was so terrified by similar bullying that she had a stroke and died.

There were also cases where landlords based their rent increases on the value of whole houses although they knew only too well that basements had been closed by the local authority; and some raised rents on houses under slum clearance orders, although they knew this to be illegal.

Of course there were landlords who fulfilled all their obligations and some who did not raise their rents at all, or who came to acceptable agreements with their tenants. But the amount of trickery was astounding; and a great deal of it, more than six years later, is still going on. See page 158.

Because the repair machinery introduced under the Rent Act is so immensely heavy and complex, this trickery is perhaps best illustrated by the personal experiences of a tenant who attempted to use that machinery against a property company with very smart agents. The tenant lives in what used to be known as an artisan's dwelling near the East London docks. The chairman of the property company lives in a neo-Georgian mansion much like that of Rachman and in the same wealthy neighbourhood. The agents have splendid new offices in Mayfair.

On 7 July 1957, the day after the Rent Act came into force, a buff envelope arrived through the letter box of a certain Mrs Bond. A merchant seaman's widow, she had been alone in the house for some years after her husband had died and her children had married. It was a nasty little house of four rooms and a scullery, clammy and dark. The landlord had done nothing whatever to it for twenty years.

When Mrs Bond went to get advice on the contents of the envelope, she was told that it was a Form A: a notice from her landlord that her rent would be going up in three months' time, and going up in two stages. During the first six months it could go up only by 7s. 6d. a week.

When this notice was checked for Mrs Bond, it was found to be charging her more than the law allowed. Because the landlord was responsible for all repairs, but not for indoor redecoration, he could charge twice the gross value of the house, plus rates. The gross value of the house was £30 a year, but he had entered it as £35. He had got the rates figure wrong too. More than fifty per cent of this landlord's notices were incorrect, and he owned well over 500 houses in that district alone.

The notice had to be returned to him, but when he sent it back with the figures corrected it had to go back yet again because he had not altered the date of issue.

That settled, Mrs Bond was asked if her house was in good

repair – a question which she evidently found wrily entertaining. She was therefore given two forms (Form G) and told that she should enter on them all the defects in her house. She first tried to do this herself, but put down items such as 'rats in the scullery' and forgot altogether to say that the back of the house badly needed to be repointed as it let in rain. She had not asked for the front door and window frames to be repainted because she felt this would be asking for the moon. But, in fact, landlords are readier to agree to this request than to any other, and many properties look from the outside, and for this reason, deceptively well maintained.

After getting some help, Mrs Bond was told to keep one of these laboriously entered forms – they have baffling headings and notes – and to send the other to her landlord. If nothing happened in the next six weeks, she should return for more advice.

Nothing, in fact, did happen. Two things, however, could have done. The landlord could have done the repairs – a most unlikely event – or he could have sent his tenant another printed notice (Form H) giving a formal undertaking to do them. In that event, Mrs Bond would have been told that the landlord was entitled to a further six months in which to honour his undertaking. She would also have learnt that if he did not do so she would be entitled to go back to her old rent and also to deduct any increases paid by then. It has to be noted, though, that if she had not taken action well within six months of getting the increase of rent notice from her landlord, she could not have gone back to her old rent, but only to $1\frac{1}{2}$ times the 1956 gross value of the house – a calculation which tenants are expected to be able to make unaided.

On the other hand, if the landlord had done some of the repairs but not all, she would have had to apply to the local authority, on a Form O, for a form P ... but more about that hideously tricky procedure later.

In Mrs Bond's case nothing happened for those first six weeks, and in most cases nothing does. A grasping landlord naturally hopes that either his tenant will not realize that further steps must be taken or that perhaps he will lose his nerve at this early stage.

Many tenants fulfil these hopes, but not Mrs Bond. As she had received no undertaking from her landlord, she duly returned for more advice – and was told that now she should apply on a Form I for a certificate of disrepair – this time to the borough council. In order to do this, she must enclose the copy of her Form G that she had kept. But although she searched everywhere she could not find it. She therefore had to start again from the beginning.

This time Form G and Form I were sent to the town hall plus a necessary postal order for 2s. 6d. – a charge made by the borough council. Mrs Bond was then told that the only two certain events of those that might now be expected were that, first, she would get a receipt for her 2s. 6d. (which she could later deduct from her rent) and, second, she could expect a visit from a public health inspector, who was almost certain to call when she was out at work; she earned £4 10s. a week as a part-time office cleaner.

This inspector, when he finally got in, would check the defects, and the council would then send her landlord a proposal to issue a certificate of disrepair. This proposal gives a landlord another three weeks' grace in which to change his mind. He will want to evade the issue of a certificate of disrepair if he can, because that will put paid to his increase of rent. This was so in the case of the property company which owned Mrs Bond's house. It gave an undertaking (this time on Form K) to do the repairs. No certificate could therefore be issued, nor could the rent be reduced.

Mrs Bond was now told that her landlord had six months in which to keep his promise. He had already gained over two months by not giving an undertaking right at the beginning, and eight and a half months naturally seemed to her altogether too long to wait especially since, by then, the rain was dripping down the electric light flex and on to her bed, and she was obliged to sleep on two chairs in the kitchen. She could, of course, and did apply to the town hall to get the roof mended, not under the Rent Act, but under the Public Health Acts. But where a landlord has already given an undertaking, the tenant is unlikely to get very far until that undertaking has expired especially if the house is found to be unfit.

At first it seemed as if Mrs Bond was going to have to wait in vain. She was already sick and tired of putting an old tin bath under the leak in the roof and having to haul it off periodically (she was not allowed to lift anything heavy after an operation) to tip its contents out of the window. Her son would have helped her if he had not emigrated to Australia, so would her daughter, if she had not been pregnant and living in Slough. Mrs Bond was sixty-seven, but many much older people frequently have to fight these battles alone.

After five and three quarter months the unbelievable happened: a man arrived to repair the roof. He was up there for exactly ten minutes and descended to say that the job was done. What he had used, said Mrs Bond, was some black stuff in a bucket, probably pitch. Her neighbour had had the same thing done by the same landlord some time ago, but a month later the rain had come in just as before.

The landlord had also had a bit of guttering re-fixed; it had been hanging down and on windy nights had clanked against the wall, keeping Mrs Bond awake; and when it rained water had cascaded into the yard. But he had not done anything about the other items on the list.

However, because he had done something, the rent could not yet be reduced. And Mrs Bond had to apply for another kind of certificate of disrepair, Form P. This necessitated another visit by a public health inspector; and as all the inspectors were up to their eyes in inspecting other disintegrating houses, none arrived for two months. So by this time the landlord, at the expense of a dab of pitch and a couple of screws, and less than an hour of a man's time, had gained nearly a year. And some landlords whose tenants do not take action so promptly gain very much more time before they suffer a reduction of rent or are forced by the local authority to do the repairs.

When Mrs Bond at last received her Form P certificate of disrepair, she had to get advice on the amount by which she could reduce her rent. She was told that she could reduce it as from the date when she applied for the certificate, two months back, and this meant some extremely complicated arithmetic, of which she would have been quite incapable on her own.

By some curious oversight, the law does not compel local

authorities to inform landlords that their tenants have been issued with these Form P certificates. And when a third person, who is advising the tenant, gives this information to the landlord and mentions what rent appears to be chargeable, the worst landlords, or their agents, often behave in the following way.

They may not answer such a letter at all – if they cannot disagree with its contents; but after the reduced rent has been in payment for several weeks or months, they will suddenly command the tenant to return his rent book to them 'for audit'. While it is with them they then write to the tenant saying that he is in considerable arrears of rent and that if these are not instantly paid up legal proceedings for eviction will be taken.

This happened to Mrs Bond. She had found the whole proceedure quite terrifying throughout, and had had to be coaxed along every inch of the way. Now she was almost out of her mind with distress. She had never in her life owed a halfpenny to anyone and now, as well as this threatening letter, her rent book had come back with arrears of £15 written across the top of the page in red ink. Anyone seeing that book, she said, would be sure to think she was dishonest. And what a dreadful thing to have to show the council if her turn ever came to be rehoused. But was it really true – could these agents really turn her out?

Although she was assured that they could not, her agitation was so great that she had to come three days in succession to be told the same thing; and, even then, she was not convinced. She said she knew it was silly, but she could not stop herself from crying. And she had not been able to keep a mouthful of food down since the letter came.

By this time, of course, the landlord had been firmly told that his tenant was in no arrears at all, having quite lawfully reduced her rent. But at this point he began to argue that he was not aware that any certificate had been issued, and he refused to listen and became abusive when referred to the letter that had told him so. The only course that remained was to tell him flatly that he could take Mrs Bond to court if he dared. He did not dare. The last thing such landlords want is for illegally entered arrears to be shown in court, and he had these quickly erased.

It is perhaps hardly believable but that is not the end either of the story or of the endurance tests that people like Mrs Bond often have to suffer.

The landlord, or rather the property company, naturally did not like receiving less than the maximum rent, and when it was clear that this could not be obtained by trickery or intimidation, the only alternative was to finish the repairs. Five months after the certificate was issued, this was done. No doubt it cost a fair amount of money but it would have cost much less if the job had been properly done much earlier. The landlord then applied for the certificate to be cancelled. But because of an even worse shortage of inspectors than before, it took four months this time to have the job passed.

Mrs Bond had been warned that she ought to put the difference between the reduced rent and the full rent aside, as the latter would be chargeable by the landlord from the date when he applied for the certificate to be cancelled. But that date was now four months back. And, in the interval, Mrs Bond had, not surprisingly, been ill. This had meant that she could no longer come for advice; and as she had not understood that the certificate had been cancelled she did not realize that for four months she should have been paying an increased rent and might at any moment be accused of being in considerable arrears. In one sense, however, her illness was fortunate. For now that she was unable to work and had nothing to live on but her pension, she had become eligible for national assistance.

In Mrs Bond's case, as in that of all tenants of controlled property, the National Assistance Board considered her rent reasonable and met it in full. Indeed, the Board does this without questioning whether the rent being charged is correct or not, in respect of repairs done or not done. This is too complicated a matter for the Board's officers to investigate. In fact, it is no one's duty to do so. The onus of finding out what ought to be paid lies entirely with the tenant, with the frequent result that the Board indirectly pays private landlords more than they are entitled to get, sometimes over very long periods.

That, however, is by the way. In Mrs Bond's case, the National Assistance Board performed a desperately needed rescue operation. Once it had been informed of the true situation, an allowance of an extra 5s. a week was made to enable Mrs Bond to pay off what she owed; and what proved even more useful, it later obtained a letter from the landlord confirming that her debt had been cleared. Had this not been done, she would yet again have had to fight off false accusations as best she could because, five months later, the landlord suddenly returned to the attack yet again and charged her with the debt that had already been confirmed as paid. At this, Mrs Bond finally lost her patience. She took a long bus ride to the agents' smart offices, stumped in, and told them, in what were no doubt embarrassing terms, precisely what she and all her neighbours thought of them. Since then she has been left in uneasy peace.

This system of obtaining repairs gives the wicked landlord many other opportunities for intimidating elderly people, and he seldom lets any of them slip. In September 1963, a certain Miss Hallett, aged seventy-eight, who had already gone through the whole Rent Act repair procedure twice because her dilapidated home had meanwhile produced a crop of new defects, received a letter from her landlord's agents addressed to *Mr* Hallett. As she was unmarried, she imagined that this must have been meant for her brother, who had long ago died, and she returned it marked 'diseased' (*sic*).

As it turned out, the agents had simply made a slip in addressing the envelope, but they immediately sent Miss Hallett the following letter.

We are writing to you since our A.R. letter addressed to Mr Hallett although it was apparently received by you was returned to us marked deceased.

We understand you refused to allow our collector to bring in your rent book today for checking and our order is for you to send in this latter in the enclosed stamped addressed envelope by return of post.

You may rest assured that this is quite safe with us and will be returned to you within a day or so, after we have had an opportunity for checking it against our records, which show that you are no less than £16 in arrear.

Alternatively, if you do not wish to do this, please telephone and make an appointment to call and bring your rent book as there is a question of your tenancy since, according to our records, this has not been devolved from Mr Hallett to you.

All this was the cruellest nonsense. First, Miss Hallett had not refused to part with her rent book – the collector had not asked her for it. Second, she could not have rested in the assurance that it would have been returned in a day or two – on the last occasion it had been held for nearly two months. Third, she was in no arrears of rent. Fourth, there was no question of her tenancy having 'devolved' from her brother or from anyone else: no member of her family had been a tenant of the house before she herself was given the tenancy at the height of the war, after being bombed out of her previous home. All the same the letter almost put her in her grave. Its accusations were instantly refuted for her by a Citizens' Advice Bureau – to which she had already had to make at least fifteen journeys – and no more has so far been heard.

In many similar cases there are grounds for prosecuting landlords. But the tenants are usually too old or timid to stand the strain. Although they now have security of tenure, they are understandably afraid that the day might come when they could lose it by a change in the law. In fact, landlords sometimes use this as a weapon for intimidation. Increasingly, too, they are pressing unwary protected tenants to sign long-term tenancy agreements which will make them, and not the landlords, responsible for repairs.

REPAIRS UNDER THE PUBLIC HEALTH ACTS

Any tenant can apply to the local public health authority (in London, the borough council) for pressure to be brought on his landlord to see to urgently needed repairs. Unknown to most tenants, the only defects that can be dealt with are those which affect health or could cause accidents. But that includes most of the major illnesses that old houses can develop.

Until 1957 there was no uncertainty about calling in 'the sanitary man' – now the public health inspector – to look at a sodden ceiling or an unusable w.c., because he represented the only hope of getting redress. But when the Rent Act enabled protected tenants to make formal applications for repairs direct to their landlords – and to resist increases of rent if these were not done – few of them realized that they could still call in 'the sanitary' in the old way and at any stage.

In one very big and insalubrious tenement block it was recently found that total confusion about this reigned. Because the landlord had only raised the controlled rents slightly, and in some cases not at all, the tenants had wrongly assumed that they could not ask him for repairs under the Rent Act. When a tenants' association was formed (five years after the passing of the Act) this was put right, and several hundred certificates of disrepair resulted. But most of the tenants still had no idea that they could also have applied for help under the Public Health Acts. And it was not until 1963 that the landlord found himself landed with a load of health notices and warnings of legal proceedings from the borough council.

What would certainly astonish these tenants, and others in the same position, is that their certificates of disrepair could not be used as a basis for legal proceedings by the borough council, or even as evidence of neglect. The certificates are issued under one Act and public health action has to be taken under another. This lack of coordination means that visits made by already harassed inspectors are often pointlessly multiplied, and urgent repairs are unnecessarily delayed. Meanwhile both house and tenant may become unfit.

Another and much more general misconception is that the recently introduced forms of compulsion can be used against all negligent landlords. In fact, they can so far only be used where houses are in multiple occupation or are occupied by more than one family – with the probable addition of tenement blocks. So the pensioner living alone in a rotting house – and indeed the vast majority of protected tenants – still have to rely on the old system.

Most tenants find this system not only confusing but profoundly disappointing. Under it, one of their worst bugbears – rising damp – cannot usually be dealt with at all, certainly not satisfactorily; and much the same applies to roofs which are so defective that they ought to be stripped and replaced. For landlords can only be required to 'remedy defects' or to 'abate nuisances', not to eradicate their cause. And the landlord who patches up a roof in such a way that it very soon lets in water again will be in little danger of further action until an inspector has actually seen it doing so. Often inspectors have to wait until there is a downpour and then tear round the houses where there have been complaints of leaks. Stained ceilings are not evidence enough because they may well have been in that condition before the last patch-up job, or the one before that.

Naturally this sort of thing is a bitter joke to the tenant. To him it seems that the local authority is either unwilling to believe him, or is on the landlord's side, or is just plain incompetent. Partly this is a matter of bad public relations. For some unguessable reason local authorities do not usually see fit to tell a tenant that they have served public health notices on his landlord. In fact, he is left completely in the dark even when his landlord is taken to court. If the builders afterwards appear, the council seldom gets the credit due to it. For the tenant can only conclude that the landlord has at last either come to his senses or unearthed his conscience.

Unknown to the tenant, however, public health inspectors have to be on very firm ground before going to court. For the wicked landlord is an extremely slippery customer. On the very day of the hearing he may merely put up a ladder and then bring his builder as a witness to say that the work is in hand. Afterwards, of course, he removes the ladder and sends his builder to another house on which there is another notice. In other cases where, for instance, there is a defective drain, the landlord may claim that the inspector himself did the damage while inspecting it.

The maximum penalty for a landlord who is successfully prosecuted under the Public Health Acts is a continuing fine of £2 a day. This has not been raised since the Acts became law nearly thirty years ago; and, even so, magistrates do not often impose it.

It is not easy for tenants, or anyone else, to understand why repairs should be dealt with under at least five different Acts (including three recent Housing Acts), or why there are so many escape hatches in all of them through which landlords can conveniently wriggle.

Now, out of this hopeless confusion, a new and alarming trouble has developed. Because the word has gone round that certain tenants (of decontrolled property) are being evicted for having called in a public health inspector, protected tenants – although in no danger of such retaliation – are becoming too afraid to ask for this help. This is particularly true of old people. They would rather, they say, let their roofs fall in than be without them.

*

What all this comes to is that where landlords are grasping and lack any sense of responsibility, private or public, they will take all possible steps to avoid having to carry out repairs to their houses, and will do so in any of the following ways:

(1) Through repair conditions in tenancy agreements and leases;

(2) by exploiting the insecurity of tenants of decontrolled (or uncontrolled) property who have no agreements;

(3) by exploiting ignorance of the complex repair rights affecting protected tenants;

(4) by the use of intimidation generally;

(5) by trickery to evade prosecution under the Public Health Acts and Housing Acts.

5 Furnished Accommodation

Furnished accommodation is a special case. It tends to produce both landlords and tenants with special characteristics. It also has a special bearing on the problem of homelessness. And all of it is uncontrolled – unless an application for control has been made to a rent tribunal by a tenant, a landlord, or a local authority under the Furnished House (Rent) Control Act of 1946. See also page 95.

For the purposes of control furnished accommodation *need not necessarily contain any furniture supplied by the landlord*. It will count as furnished if the rent includes payment for services, or if any room, such as a kitchen, is shared with the landlord. The law says that this must date from before 6 July 1957, but sharing is often interpreted as a service. 'Service' in this sense includes the provision of cleaning, lighting, or heating, but excludes 'board' or charges for meals, if these represent a sizeable proportion of the rent. 'Furniture' usually includes those bits of it which, although fixed to the walls, can easily be removed without damage to them.

FEELINGS OF ISOLATION

Furnished accommodation is much more scattered and various than any other kind and the tenant often finds himself in quite a different boat from that of his neighbours. He may be on his own in an area where all the other houses are occupied by their owners, or in a street where everyone else – although in identical houses – pays a controlled rent and to a different landlord. Only in blocks of furnished flats, or in houses split up for furnished letting, is he likely to have any feeling of solidarity or any means of comparing his conditions. Unless he lives in a luxury flat, his landlord is much less likely to be a property company than a private individual, and one with whom – for better or worse – he will probably have a good deal of contact.

The fact that, in this case, the tenant is not only living in someone else's house, but among someone else's possessions, makes his position particularly unenviable – and this quite apart from the strong probability that his taste and the landlord's will totally differ.

FEES AND CHARGES

The tenant who hears of a vacancy in furnished accommodation through an agent may have to pay a fee for the introduction and may also be charged the equivalent of a month's rent, or more, with or without further sums as key money or as a premium or deposit, very often in cash and without a receipt. He may also have to pay a deposit against any damage he may do.

The landlord may also make a charge, and it can be a very heavy one, for fixtures and fittings. Even if the latter consist of a single electric light bulb this can still be done.

In one case the father of a big family had to pay, in all, £350 before he was allowed entry to a four-room house in a shocking state of repair, and without a bathroom, in an industrial district.

There is at present no limit to the kind or the amount of charges with which a prospective tenant of furnished accommodation can be faced.

TENANCY AGREEMENTS*

The tenant has no legal right to an agreement. The better the quality of the accommodation, and of the furniture, however, the more likely he is to get one, with one exception: he will almost certainly not get one if he is going to live in a house where the owner also lives, as the latter will naturally not want to tie himself down to a tenant whom he may later find uncongenial, or worse.

*See also pages 58, 59, 60, and 61.

THE FURNITURE

The better the furniture and fittings are, the more terrified the tenant will be of damaging them. If he has an agreement, and an inventory, he may find himself faced, when his time is up, with crippling bills because his children have scratched a valuable table, or spilt ink on the carpet, or drawn their own designs on the wallpaper.

At the other end of the scale the furniture, consisting perhaps of a bed, a chair, and a table, may be worthless junk, and there may be nothing on the floor but a strip of battered linoleum. Yet simply because of these miserable trappings, the tenant can be charged a high uncontrolled rent; for landlords are under no obligation about the kind or amount of furniture they supply.

THE TENANT

The tenant of furnished accommodation may be very rich or almost destitute. What makes him different from all other tenants is that he is nearly always a bird of passage. He usually has to take furnished accommodation either because he needs only a temporary refuge, or because he cannot find anything unfurnished, or because he cannot afford furniture of his own. For these last two reasons thousands of young couples have to start married, or unmarried, life in furnished rooms, and they usually find the rents so high that they cannot save for furniture of their own and, in any case, have nowhere to keep it.

WHY FURNISHED ACCOMMODATION IS AVAILABLE

Furnished accommodation is much easier to find, at a price, than unfurnished. The reasons for this are very complicated. Some landlords believe that if they let furnished they will be less likely to find themselves saddled with troublesome tenants. Some feel that a tenant who has his own furniture would be more difficult to remove than one who only has a suitcase. Landlords who let rooms in their own homes usually have enough furniture for their tenants and may be reluctant to get rid of it anyway. But an important reason for furnished accommodation being easier to find than unfurnished is that tenants do not generally stay long of their own accord, and can of course be given notice if they cause the slightest damage to the furniture or the smallest inconvenience to their landlords.

FURNISHED ROOMS IN OWNER-OCCUPIED HOUSES

This quick turnover of tenants occurs particularly in owner-occupied houses. Here the landlord is probably letting rooms only because he cannot afford to do otherwise. No one in his senses would sacrifice his privacy or endanger his possessions for any other reason – unless he happened to be extraordinarily unselfish. Naturally, then, this house-owner is inclined to be more selective than any other landlord about what kind of tenant he takes, and will usually jib at taking people with children (dogs may be more acceptable), or people who are likely to hang about the house all day, or coloured people whom he will suspect of having outlandish habits. If, however, he happens to be coloured himself he will be far more free and easy about whom he takes. But dark-skinned landlords are, of course, in a very small minority; and the childless tenant of furnished rooms in an owner-occupied house usually has a white landlord or lady – probably a middle-aged or elderly widow. Because this is so, she will naturally want to make rules for her own convenience and protection. But because the tenant's position is so perilous, and rather more so than that of his opposite number in unfurnished rooms, he can be even more intensively persecuted.

Causes of Friction: Traps and Tyrannies

The tenant of furnished rooms in a house where the owner also lives has to be particularly careful about the amount of electricity he uses if he has no separate meter. His landlord can charge for electricity at whatever rate he likes and can include this charge in the rent. This can amount to much more than the tenant would have to pay otherwise, but all the same he can often be made to feel he is cheating if he uses electricity for anything but light. He is quite likely to be given notice if he buys an electric fire or uses an electric iron. On the other hand if he has a meter the landlord can, quite lawfully, have it fixed at a higher rate than normal, so that the tenant constantly feels he is being cheated. Tenants frequently get notice to quit simply for questioning electricity or gas charges – rates charges too.

It hardly needs to be added that shared bathrooms, telephones, and kitchens – or indeed anything shared at all – will be liable to cause ructions – and sooner or later expulsion.

Of course the landlord has to protect himself from exploitation. But with his power to give four weeks' notice and his ability very quickly to find a replacement, he may impose totally unreasonable restrictions, coupled with threats (just as he also might in the less likely event of letting his rooms unfurnished). For instance he may insist that the tenant goes to bed early and does not get up earlier than he does himself, even if the tenant's job demands that he should. The tenant may be barred from entertaining friends or relatives, except at certain times, or altogether. He may be barred particularly from inviting coloured friends. If he is ill or unable to work for some other reason, he may be forbidden to apply for national assistance because this will mean an official visit to the house and the asking of certain searching questions which for various reasons may be extremely unwelcome.

The tenant may not be evicted for disobeying any of these orders – although there are innumerable cases where this *has* happened. Instead, sanctions may be applied. He can find that his washing line has mysteriously disappeared, or that the electric light bulbs in his room have been taken out, or that the blankets have gone from his bed.

In fact the tenant can lose his liberty completely, and his privacy too. His landlord may reserve the right to come into his room whenever he likes – quite unlawfully since he takes rent for it and is therefore trespassing – on the grounds that he owns the house and all it contains. He can behave as if he owns the tenant too.

Children

Unless he has the motherly type of landlady, by far the most dangerous thing that the tenant of furnished rooms can do is to start a family, partly because of the very natural fear of disturbance, and partly because small children are no respecters of furniture.

Over half the families who become homeless, in London at any rate, have been evicted from furnished rooms; and a very usual reason is that the wives have recently had their first or second babies.

Even to be expecting a baby can be fatal, and has, if humanly possible, to be concealed. If this succeeds, and the baby is born in hospital, the mother is often driven to try to smuggle it into the house at night and to take it out again very early in the morning, in the pathetic hope that its existence will not be noticed.

Can Anything Be Done?

Nothing whatever can be done to prevent this kind of intimidation because, where there is no control, or security of tenure, the landlord can make what rules he pleases. He will naturally tend to make more where the demand for housing is highest. Some of the rules may be made because of previous bitter experience. All the same his power tends to make him a tyrant.

THE OWNER ELSEWHERE: STILL WORSE TREATMENT

If the owner of the house lives somewhere else there will obviously be less day-to-day friction, but the tenant can suffer even worse treatment. This can go to particularly shocking lengths when practised on visitors to this country who are desperate for a refuge – as shown in a letter recently published in the *Sunday Times* from a visiting professor. On arriving in London with his family, all he could find was a room plus what had been advertised as a kitchen – which turned out to be 'a space about a yard square behind a tattered curtain'. The rent for this was 'exorbitant', but, he wrote, 'the worst iniquity was an electricity meter into which shillings had to be placed, it seemed, every few minutes, or the lights went out'. That, however, was only his first experience.

Astounded to find that it was 'perfectly legal for landlords to adjust meters', he and his family moved to another so-called flat which had been advertised, in the usual jargon, as particularly desirable. 'Here again', his letter goes on, 'we ran into such mean tricks that I had to obtain the assistance of my solicitor to get me out. One trick was that although I had paid a substantial deposit to obtain the flat (which again consisted really only of a single room) and had expressly stated that I needed it only for a very few days, threatening attempts were made on our first night of occupation to force me to pay for a much longer period in advance: meanwhile they would retain the deposit "against breakages". Another trick involved the confiscation and locking up of our youngest child's rather costly new go-cart when I failed to yield to these attempts and also to acknowledge indebtedness for various additional charges of which I had not previously heard. About these matters I had to call the police who seemed unwilling to take any part.'

In London this kind of experience is not at all uncommon.

LEAVING FURNISHED ACCOMMODATION

The tenant who has no solicitor to rescue him can much more easily pack up and go than he could if the furniture was his own. Landlords often complain that they have not been given four weeks' notice, but they just as often fail to give this themselves when getting a tenant out. See also page 60.

Length of Notice

Time after time, tenants are wrongly informed by their landlords – sometimes out of ignorance, sometimes not – that they are entitled to only one week's notice to quit simply because their rooms are furnished.

There is, however, much more genuine ignorance of the law among landlords of low-rated furnished rooms than among most others – and for a special reason. As they are so frequently letting rooms in their own homes, and doing so because they have no other way of inducing ends to meet, they tend to avoid consulting solicitors for fear of excessive costs. Many of them were letting rooms long before the Rent Act was passed, when only one week's notice was needed. Newcomers to this country who become landlords have often lived previously in furnished rooms and very understandably but quite unlawfully give their tenants the same short notice as they themselves received.

Locking Out and Turning Out

There is a very widespread belief that tenants of furnished rooms can be locked out without any breach of the law. But if this is done while the tenant's notice to quit or his temporary security of tenure (granted by a rent tribunal) have not expired, it is unlawful.

A tenant who finds himself locked out should lose no time at all in consulting a solicitor. There are various forms of legal action which can be taken, and it has quite often happened that a landlord has had to re-admit a tenant on the same day as he locked him out rather than be sued and have to pay heavy damages.

On the other hand, there have been cases where the landlord afterwards made life unendurable for the tenant either by extreme personal persecution, or by cutting off water, light, and gas. Again, if this happens, the tenant should go straight to a solicitor, taking a witness if possible. The landlord can certainly be sued. So he can be, too, if he puts any of the tenant's belongings outside the house and they are damaged or lost, or if his belongings and clothes are inside his rooms and the landlord either removes them or refuses to let the tenant fetch them.

There are some circumstances in which a landlord might not find himself liable for damages if he turned a tenant out *after* his security of tenure (minimum four weeks) has expired. But any solicitor would most strongly advise him not to do this – and to get a court order for eviction instead – because the risks involved, especially if force is used, are very great.

One tenant of furnished rooms, the father of four children,

came home after shopping with his family to find the landlord changing the lock on the front door. When he protested and tried to push his way in, the landlord slashed his arm with the screwdriver he had been using; and in the uproar that followed his wife, who was pregnant, was punched in the stomach by the landlord's wife. That landlord afterwards found himself in prison as well as liable for damages.

Tenants of furnished rooms get this kind of treatment more often than any others. But although they have redress in law, they do not always get it, because the landlord frequently turns out to be a man of too small means to be worth suing. Besides, a family which is locked out is usually far too busy looking for somewhere to sleep the night to consult a solicitor; and a family which is homeless and split up usually prefers to cut its losses. (See also page 132.)

RENT BOOKS

Although the weekly tenant of furnished rooms has the same right as any other to a properly entered rent book, he much less often gets one; and he cannot be advised to complain because of his insecure position. The landlord is usually hoping to evade income tax.

In a small furnished house in East London where there were three tenants (one of whom – with his family – had been there for six years) it was recently found that no rent books had been supplied and no receipts had been given for rent, with the result that the tenants had no means of proving their right to be there. The owner was thought – even by the local rates office – to be a woman who lived near by; but behind her was a property company which had deceived its own solicitor about the way the house was run. Rent books were supplied just in time for the landlord to apply to the courts for an eviction order.

APPEAL TO A RENT TRIBUNAL

Whether the tenant has another right entirely depends on the rateable value of his home. If its value on 6 November 1956 was £40 or less in London, or £30 elsewhere in England and Wales, he has a right to apply to a rent tribunal on the ground that his rent is excessive; and in certain circumstances (see the beginning of this chapter) he has this right even if his rooms were let to him unfurnished. To use it, however, can land him in serious difficulty and danger, and to make this clear it is necessary to give some idea of procedure.

Applying to a Rent Tribunal

When a tenant goes to the offices of a rent tribunal he is given a form on which he enters details about his tenancy: how many rooms he has, what furniture the landlord provides, what rooms are shared with him, and so on.

If the tenant's application is accepted, the rent of his rooms can be considered by the tribunal whether or not he has already received a valid notice to quit.

The landlord is sent a similar form; and soon afterwards a visit is made to the house to check the information given by both sides and to note conditions generally, so that the tribunal can have as much information as possible on which to judge the rent.

There is no standard method of determining whether a rent is excessive or not (see also page 123). Each rent tribunal is free to use what method it thinks best.

Representation and Costs

Both landlord and tenant are asked to attend the hearing of the case and both can be legally represented; but there is no provision for this under legal aid. Badly-off landlords and tenants who pass a means test can be inexpensively represented through a Legal Advice Centre (see page 23).

Rent After the Verdict

If the tribunal decides that the rent should be lower than it is, the landlord cannot afterwards lawfully charge more for the accommodation concerned than the tribunal decides, and still cannot do so even after the tenant who is occupying it at the time of the hearing has left. Information about reduction is sent by the tribunal to the local authority, which has the power to prosecute the landlord if the rent he charges is higher than that which a rent tribunal has fixed. But tenants cannot risk reporting this. Recently it was found that £6 was being charged for one room, the rent of which had been fixed at 30s. per week.

Security

If a tenant has *not* received a valid notice to quit when he applies to a rent tribunal, he immediately becomes protected against eviction at least until the hearing of the case. A notice to quit served after the tenant is under tribunal protection is invalid.

Rent tribunals also have the power to grant temporary security of tenure, usually for three months, but this can be extended if the family still has not found somewhere else to live and makes another application.

Difficulties

For Landlords. In a very high proportion of cases brought before rent tribunals, in cities at any rate, the landlords are newcomers to this country – or comparatively so – and they tend to be young and inexperienced and ignorant of the law.

Among the landlords of low-rated furnished rooms there are, as in any other department of rented housing, many out-and-out scoundrels. But these are usually too clever to get themselves involved with rent tribunals. Their tenants are often forbidden, as a condition of their tenancies, to apply to a tribunal, and are subject to such fierce intimidation that they would not dare to do so. In other cases the tribunal may find itself quite unable to establish who the landlord is.

The landlord who most often finds himself caught usually owns only one house in which he lives himself. He is, however, the antithesis of the respectable middle-aged landlady who lets rooms in her own house. Unlike her, he frequently charges rents which though fairly low in themselves can be very high indeed in relation to the kind of accommodation he provides; and he also tends to be unselective about his tenants and unconcerned about the number of children they have.

This landlord's house is usually vilely overcrowded and the furniture is shoddy fifth-hand stuff. There are none of the trappings of respectable furnished rooms – no divan beds with fitted covers, no standard lamps, bedside tables, or polished wardrobes for children to wreck. But that is not the only reason why this landlord welcomes children. In his country private property is not nearly so sacred as it is here; children are very far from being regarded as liabilities; and he probably has a good many himself.

Because this is so often the coloured landlord's attitude towards children, and because he crams as many families in as his house will hold (far too many in the eyes of the health authorities), he does a very great deal, unconsciously or not, to prevent total homelessness. This is far too little recognized. So is his need to charge more than his rooms are worth, which usually arises from being driven to buy a house which he cannot afford. (See also page 70.)

In fact he usually finds himself a landlord by accident rather than design and does not at all enjoy the experience. As a beginner, and in chaotic conditions, he tends to meet every crisis by threatening expulsion – with or without violence.

Of course there are endless variations of this pattern. It can be quite uncoloured, or the colours may be reversed. The landlord may be under no financial pressure himself, or he may continue to charge high rents after such pressure has ceased. Very possibly he is saving up to bring his elder children or parents over from his own country. But he may not even be aware that he is overcharging, and this is no wonder because he has no rules to go by and no example to follow but that of other landlords.

For Tenants. The tenant's sufferings here need far less explanation. Unlike the tenant of unfurnished rent-controlled accommodation, he is nearly always young. But he is vulnerable in a way that older people are not, because everything that affects him affects, to an even more painful degree, his wife and children. Although he is thankful not to be homeless, he feels that he is being mercilessly exploited, and he resents this with equal passion if the landlord is a citizen of his own country or if he is not. That he and his landlord may, in a sense, both be refugees does not (very understandably) occur to him.

This typical tenant is usually unaware of the purpose or even the existence of rent tribunals until, after a furious quarrel with his landlord, he sees eviction looming – and takes advice. He tends to be less interested in the tribunal's power to reduce his rent than in its ability to grant him temporary security, especially if, for instance, his wife is expecting a baby. If he is coloured, eviction will be an even worse fate than if he is not. Probably he will have to leave a neighbourhood where he may at last have managed to get himself accepted after years of hostility; and his wife, who when homeless may be separated from him, will find this a much more terrifying prospect than she would in her own country.

This tenant rarely applies to a rent tribunal out of any feeling of vindictiveness against his landlord and is very apprehensive about the result. His motive is pure desperation. But he feels immense satisfaction that he has a right to apply and that his case will afterwards be thoroughly investigated.

Dangers After Application

Any landlord faced with rent tribunal intervention is bound to have very hard feelings against the tenant who has brought this about, and quite naturally will not want to keep him a moment longer than he has to. It is not merely that the rent of his room may be permanently reduced, although that is bad enough. He does not want his house to be inspected, and perhaps not only from the point of view of his personal privacy. It could easily be that, taking his rent in cash, he has not declared the full amount to the tax authorities. To make this safer he may not have provided any of his tenants with rent books or even receipts. All this and certain other dubious arrangements or activities, punishable by law, could – he very rightly thinks – now come to light. At the very least the overcrowding and lack of repairs and conveniences could be discovered by the health authorities. In any case he has everything to lose and nothing at all to gain. There have been cases where a tribunal has increased a rent, but they are extremely rare.

Retaliation by the Landlord. The tenant who applies to a rent tribunal does not expect his landlord to accept this quietly.

The important point here, which is usually missed by critics of the system – because they so rarely meet either the tenants or the landlords concerned – is that in 99 per cent of cases they have already fallen out, and that it is chiefly because the tenant feared eviction that he made his application in the first place. This can be said to be a misuse of his right to have his rent considered, but in nearly all instances his rent is in fact found excessive; and, in any case, a tenant faced with family homelessness can hardly be expected not to seize on any means of getting temporary security.

If this tenant first takes advice he will be warned – or he ought to be – about probable retaliation, and that a tribunal's written verdict granting temporary security is not necessarily going to act as a passport to his home, as he might well have hoped. He has to be told that he must be prepared to find himself locked out or thrown out, and that it will be of little use to appeal to the police if this happens.

Police Protection?

What makes the tenant of furnished rooms more insecure than any other is that he can be locked out and his few possessions put out with the minimum trouble to the landlord. If he had his own furniture the police might take a more serious view of his inability to get at it, since property offences in the eyes of the law are apparently more serious than any others.

This, too, is why the police tend to side with the landlord rather than the tenant in any dispute in which they are allowed to intervene. But in London, at any rate, they are under orders not to intervene in tenancy disputes unless violence is used.

A tenant who shows the police the verdict of a rent tribunal granting him security of tenure, and tells them that he is nevertheless threatened with violent expulsion, is likely to be disillusioned if he hopes for their protection. He will probably be told that the police cannot intervene simply on the unproved evidence of a verbal threat, but that they should, of course, be called at once if violence actually takes place. This is extremely chilly comfort to a tenant who fears that the violence may involve his wife and children.

Not long ago violence of this kind was expected by a family (which was under the protection of a tribunal) consisting of a married couple, three small children, and their grandmother. The landlord, who was not a coloured man, had already carried out the same threat against another family in the house, with the help of two strong-arm thugs. And he had done this on the day (it was the day on which he always collected rents) and at the time that he had said he would.

In order to prevent this happening twice, the police were informed and were all the more urgently asked for help because the mother of the children was a polio cripple. They said that they were extremely sorry but they could not afford the time or the men. The right thing would be for the family to telephone if help was actually needed. If they had no telephone there would be a box not far away.

The landlord's threat was duly carried out. The children were dragged from their beds, the father knocked down, and their mother and grandmother dumped on the pavement. A photograph was taken of them there by a press photographer.

Preventive Action

When a tenant who is technically under the protection of a rent tribunal is threatened with violent expulsion he usually asks for advice.

As in many other cases, it has been found extremely useful to have a solicitor's letter sent immediately to his landlord, warning him against breaking the law. Anyone other than a solicitor who writes direct to the landlord risks an accusation of interfering between him and his tenant. But if no solicitor is available – which frequently happens in an emergency, especially after office hours – it has also been found effective to give the tenant a similar letter, but addressed to himself and in non-legal language, which he can then show to his landlord.

This works particularly well with inexperienced landlords who are unaware that they are risking any penalties, financial or otherwise. But what can be more useful is a little diplomatic negotiation before this very dangerous stage. If a tenant has already applied to a rent tribunal but immediately afterwards tells his landlord that he is willing to withdraw his application if only he can be allowed to live in peace, the landlord may be only too happy to agree, and in fact often is. He may have imagined that his tenant was utterly helpless, and he may not have had the slightest idea of the powers of rent tribunals. If he can avoid having his rent reduced by keeping the present tenant on, the chances are that he will do so. And relations between them are quite likely to be improved because both have made concessions.

This is one good reason for extending the right to apply to rent tribunals. And this is yet another example of the tortuous and crafty methods which have to be found to prevent families from becoming unnecessarily homeless.

*

To sum up very broadly:

The tenant of furnished rooms is particularly dependent on the character of his landlord because they so often live at close quarters.

He frequently gets illegally short notice, seldom a rent book, and usually excessive electricity and other charges.

If his children are accepted his landlord is likely to be coloured and the house overcrowded or the rent prohibitively high.

If he exercises his unique right to apply to a rent tribunal he risks retaliation, but gains a bargaining counter.

6 Misjudgements and Misconceptions

Landlords, as a class, evidently feel that they are badly mis-judged not only by their tenants but also by the public. One of the declared aims of their new joint council is to put this right. Certainly the very word 'landlord' suggests wealth, power, and privilege, which are not by any means always present. And the immigrant for whom landlordism can be the only alternative to homelessness is not the only case in point.

Among old people there are many very minor landlords who are poorer than their tenants. And there are others who, after having to leave their homes to live and work elsewhere, have found that they could not regain possession of them because the courts held that greater hardship would be caused to the tenants by evicting them, especially those with children, than to the landlord by refusing his claim.

There is no doubt, either, that the level at which rents were controlled before 1957 caused hardship to the landlord who owned only one or two rented houses and had no other source of income. He may simply have made an unlucky investment of small savings or have been landed with his house by inheritance; and, either way, selling may not have been a feasible solution because, in areas of declining population particularly, a house let to protected tenants can fail altogether to find a buyer.

Elderly and poorly-off landlords exist in surprisingly great numbers. But whereas each may have only a very few tenants, one big-scale property owner may have thousands. And he is likely to be completely out of touch with them, not only because he has never met them, but because he has no personal ex-perience of their difficulties – or prefers to put his own modest beginnings well behind him.

In his remoteness from the people whose homes he owns, the modern big-scale urban landlord is quite unlike the benevolent country squire, who certainly still exists. And aware of the total lack of respect in which he is held, he tends to defend himself by attacking his tenants and representing them as a worthless lot. Rather naturally, these attacks are chiefly concentrated on those of his tenants who occupy, like permanent fixtures, his rent-controlled properties. He goes as far as to accuse them of 'exploiting' him by their failure voluntarily to remove themselves, and of being no better than 'squatters'. But when using this very powerful propaganda he seldom mentions the very important fact that these highly objectionable tenants are chiefly both old and poor.

Perhaps that sounds rather sweeping. But if these tenants had not been poor, they would scarcely have chosen to live, and to go on living, in the lowest-rated houses. For the low assessment of their value usually means that such houses are small and lacking in conveniences, such as bathrooms, and exist in the least desirable districts – very often the grimmest industrial districts of cities.

Of course limited rents and security against eviction are bound to be a discouragement to moving. But the Rent Act did not provide any extra accommodation and, since its passing, poor and elderly protected tenants have found themselves trapped. Only people with private means or who are still earning and have wives who work as well can pay high decontrolled rents to get themselves civilized or even tolerable flats. The chief hope of this for their pension-dependent seniors is the arrival of the bulldozer to demolish their homes. With very few exceptions this is longed for as a miraculous deliverance, because it will mean a modern council flat or bed-sitting room at a rent which will suit their pockets, and under a landlord who may impose certain restrictions but whom at least they can trust.

Those who have stayed on in rent-controlled property very often live alone because their children have grown up and have sought their own front doors. And because women outlive men – and also because so many men in the last fifty years have been killed in war – a great many of them are widows.

These are the tenants who are often represented by landlords, and by certain economists, as selfishly taking up more space than they need. Yet these very landlords do their utmost to prevent such tenants from sub-letting their vacant rooms (thus very often causing the National Assistance Board to pay more in rent allowances than would otherwise be necessary); and these houses with their 'unfairly' low rents have, in thousands of cases, been their tenants' homes, if not since they were born, at least since they were married or after they were bombed out of similar houses during the war. In fact, it is not unusual to find that such tenants have lived in their present homes, and have gone on and on faithfully paying rent, for over half a century. And it is rare to find that the houses they live in are not nearly twice as old as that. Usually they are in a state of advanced senility, if not of near-collapse.

In this typical situation the respective interests of the owner and the owned inevitably clash, and ideas of what is fair differ strikingly.

HOW THE TENANT SEES IT

An elderly tenant in a house of this kind usually blames the agent – with very little malice and a good deal of humour – for the sins of the landlord, because the agent's name is the only one he knows. It is on his rent book. But as he does not know the agent personally he has the feeling of being under remote control – which is both alarming and frustrating.

Unable to show the defects in his house to anyone but the rent-collector, who rarely has time or inclination to look at them, and unable to get any answers to his letters, he has long been painfully aware that he is a person of no consequence whatever except as a payer of rent – and one whom the landlord would dearly like to remove, or see dead, because his rent is controlled.

If this tenant is allowed to sub-let – or, rather, cannot lawfully be prevented from doing so – he usually disdains to charge his sub-tenant more than half his own rent. He still does this after it has been pointed out to him that, with new sub-tenants, taken on since the Rent Act came into force, he could charge what he likes. To make a profit, especially out of such shabby and poky accommodation, would, as he sees it, be doing down people who desperately need homes. It would also be a form of cheating which could ruin the good name which is one of the most precious of his few possessions.

Because this is his point of view he is quite unable to understand his landlord's greed or the total lack of concern which this nameless, invisible, and immensely powerful person evidently has for his own reputation. Another thing that is beyond him is that although this landlord must be fairly rolling in money he has extraordinarily little sense for someone in his position. A sensible man would never let his properties rot.

Living in a decaying house which is not his own, this typical tenant would feel very strongly disinclined to get any of the repairs done himself, even if he could afford to do so. For he can see no sense in taking on what is the landlord's responsibility on top of paying rent and rates.

On the other hand the tenant is anything but clear about what, exactly, is his landlord's responsibility. He had always thought, for instance, and goes on doing so, that the landlord is totally responsible for the upkeep of his house. It stands to reason that he should be. So if he, the tenant, does his best to brighten up the place with a bit of wallpaper and paint, he is convinced that he is doing his landlord a favour. He does not realize that, unless the landlord chooses otherwise, the tenant is responsible for indoor decoration. But how should he know that? Although certain terms (unsigned) may be printed in his rent book, this often refers to housing Acts of ten or twenty years ago – and anyway the language used is gibberish to him.

This typical tenant speaks as he finds with remarkable fairness. If he happens to have a good landlord he will say so, without being asked, to anyone whom he may be consulting. If his landlord owns only one or two houses, he acknowledges that it must be very expensive to keep them in order – though he does rather wonder why he bought them in the first place and why he does not sell them now, with prices as high as they are. Also he quite freely admits that the rent of his home is very low – as rents go nowadays. And, because of this, he would be perfectly willing to pay more, according to what he could afford, in exchange for the minimum of convenience and, above all, for a watertight roof and firm, dry walls.

As things are, and as his new wallpaper, put up by a son or a grandson, comes unstuck in less than a month or shows great sodden patches, he gives up trying – usually he did so years ago. And there are other discouragements. The better the look of the house, the worse his chances of being rehoused. Also, where the tenant, in desperation, does repairs for which the landlord has made himself responsible under the 1957 Rent Act, that landlord can charge the maximum controlled rent – most unfairly in the tenant's view – as if he had done the repairs himself.

What the tenant would really enjoy would be for the landlord to spend a night or two in the house and see how he liked it and what good it did his health. But on the whole he accepts his own discomfort with a remarkable lack of bitterness.

THE LANDLORD'S POINT OF VIEW

When a private landlord is responsible for repairs he, in his turn, is bound to feel resentment against his tenant. He naturally sees every repair that he is asked to do as a potential chip off his profits, and he puts up a stiff resistance to doing any at all unless obliged by law.

To him, this bothersome tenant ought to be properly grateful to have a roof over his head. But as well as being ungrateful, he is evidently a person completely lacking in responsibility and initiative. He will not even drive in a nail if he thinks he can get the landlord to do it for him. He is continually pestering about quite unimportant matters, such as broken sashcords (too bad if he can't open the window or if it comes rushing down on his hand), and he has absolutely no idea about labour shortages or costs, or about taxation. He seems to imagine that his landlord is made of money or is in the property business for charity or for fun.

Another thing that riles the landlord is that the tenant seems to think he has a right to decent conditions, although he pays far less than the economic rent for the house. Of course the tenant is not responsible for rent control, but no matter.

This pest of a tenant may even go as far as to ask for the tap in the yard to be brought inside the house and fixed above his sink. He is not the man his father or grandfather was. They never complained about having to go out to fetch every drop of water in every kind of weather.

And then there is the sink itself. Why, in heaven's name, should the landlord be expected to supply a 'butler's sink' when the old one which has been there for fifty years or more still holds water? The same goes for the old 'kitchener' stove which the tenant claims smokes him out, and for the w.c. outside, which he says is not much better than a broken-down hen house. As for damp walls, does he really expect the landlord to put in a damp course? Usually the tenant does not go as far as to ask for a bath, and that is just as well. Of course there are grants to be had from the local authority to put in improvements such as bathrooms, indoor w.c.s, hot-water systems, ventilated larders, and goodness knows what else; and the tenant may be willing to pay the extra rent lawfully chargeable on such improvements, as well as extra rates; but what he does not seem to realize is that the landlord will have to pay half the bill – more if the grant limit is exceeded – yet isn't free to do as he likes with the house for years afterwards.

In fact, so the argument continues, the tenant does not even try to see his landlord's difficulties. He may pay the rent promptly enough and, for all that anyone knows, he may keep the place spotless too and generally behave himself quite respectably. But he is hopelessly uncooperative.

For instance, he was given the chance of buying his house some years ago and at a very reasonable figure, considering that he was the sitting tenant. One might think he would jump at the chance, but what does he do? He rushes off and gets advice – no doubt from some quite unqualified person – and then has the nerve to say that, much as he would like to own a house, he does not want this one at any price. He is afraid (people these days are always afraid of something) that the repairs will cost too much. But he doesn't mind, and never has, what they cost his unfortunate landlord.

I have had to listen to such arguments over and over again, and it is remarkable how little they differ. What is equally surprising is that no matter whom they may be addressing, landlords – quite unlike tenants, who have never been in positions of power – always seem confident of complete sympathy and agreement. They are also apt to believe, without any inquiry, that the elderly tenants whom they long to remove would find it a happy solution to dump themselves on relatives, and that they all have such relatives with spare rooms ready to receive them.

Invariably, too, landlords fall back on the perfectly true fact that wages have risen quite disproportionately to controlled rents. But they tend to leave out of this argument two rather essential points: that the majority of their controlled tenants are no longer earning, and that in addition to rent they have to pay rates. The latter point is all the more important because in poor districts the rate in the pound is often surprisingly high. To live in a house with a low rateable value can nevertheless mean that rates add as much as one third to the rent, and both may have to come out of a single pension.

As landlords become increasingly unpopular, especially those free to charge what they like, their accusations against their tenants get wilder and more damaging. One London landlord, against whom public demonstrations were held for evicting a family (who owed him about £3), turned on his critics and accused them of total ignorance of the wicked tricks that tenants get up to. He did not go as far as to say that these tricks can make landlords homeless or destitute, but held that they are so various and widespread that he could write a book about them. He then cited the case of a fatherless family out of whom for many weeks he had got no rent before he was able to have them turned out by the bailiffs.

It could be that the mother of this family deliberately refused to pay the rent. But neither its height, nor her income, were so much as mentioned. Perhaps the landlord held that both were irrelevant, and that if she could not afford the rent she should not have taken it on. But was she already on her own when the tenancy began? And, if not, how had her income been affected by bereavement or desertion?

These are the kind of questions that ought to be considered if tenants are not to be condemned out of hand. Eviction is, after all, an extremely heavy sentence. Yet because so many cases, where decontrolled property is concerned, never reach the courts, the sole judge is often the landlord.

REASONS FOR ARREARS

The one thing that every tenant knows is that if he fails in his rent he runs the risk of eviction.

Under the present desperate shortage of housing, no tenant in his senses wilfully endangers himself and his family in this way. The tenant who does so is usually out of his senses or at least in a very disturbed state of mind – often due to some agonizing anxiety or distress which has temporarily overwhelmed him. Quite as often, however, he may simply be unable to produce the money.

The average landlord, naturally infuriated at not getting his rent, would not be very likely to accept either of these reasons even if they were put to him. He would probably see them as mere excuses and pretty thin ones at that. But often they are not put to him, or not until the arrears have been mounting up for weeks, by which time he will be in a disturbed state of mind himself and will probably have issued a notice to quit. He then blames the tenant for not contacting him earlier, quite forgetting that his own practice is not to answer, or perhaps even read, his tenants' letters.

It could be that, even so, the landlord will hold his hand if the reason for arrears sounds like genuine illness. He may do this simply out of sympathy; or he may do it because he knows that a court might not think fit to grant an eviction order, in which case he would lose the costs of his claim. For if his property is rent-controlled the case he puts to the court must be a reasonable one, whereas if it is decontrolled the tenant has no such protection. This, indeed, is one reason why some tenants are evicted if they owe as little as £3 or £4 while others owing ten times as much are, in rare cases, not even taken to court.

But the reason for arrears which is practically never accepted is that the tenant simply cannot produce the money. That, in the landlord's view, is just plain nonsense. No one is as poor as that nowadays or, if they are, it must be their own fault. Haven't we got a welfare state? Of course, so the landlord argues, the tenant has the money to pay: the trouble is that the welfare state has made him soft, taken away his sense of responsibility, and, if the truth were only known, he has probably spent his rent money in the pubs or at the dogs.

That, of course, could be true. But it is certainly and emphatically not true that the welfare state invariably ensures that the tenant has the means to pay.

Poverty While Earning

Low wages are the most obvious cause of rent arrears. Even in London, where wages are much higher than anywhere else, it is not at all uncommon to find that the father of a family, as its sole supporter, is earning only £11 or £12 a week gross. Of course there will be family allowances for the children. If there are two of them the allowance will be 8s. a week, and for every extra child another 10s. But the value of these has long ago been devoured by rising prices, especially for fares, food, coal, and electricity. And there can be considerable poverty for the family on £12 a week or less, even if the rent is only £2 a week and there are no other commitments in the way of hire purchase or private insurance. A hard winter and a high electricity bill can mean choosing between paying the landlord or being plunged into freezing darkness, and perhaps just at a time when there is illness in the family or a new baby, with all its expensive needs, has arrived.

But thousands of low earners, doing absolutely essential work which is often either dirty or dangerous or both, are of course having to pay much more than £2 a week in rent even for the most sordid family accommodation, if it is decontrolled. And in London, in 1963, the Family Service Units made a survey and found that practically no tolerable private accommodation was on offer to families with children at less than £6 a week exclusive of rates – £8 to £10 was the usual minimum.

The alternatives faced by low-earning families on rents beyond their means can often lie between falling into arrears or reducing standards below what can be tolerated. Increasingly, parents in this position are becoming desperate at their inability to feed their children properly; and immigrants sometimes remark in bewilderment that even in their own countries they never found themselves in quite such painful straits.

It has to be remembered, too, that where there is only one child there will be no family allowance; that where children are under five years old there will be no school dinners; that the poorest families get no benefit from tax allowance for children; and that where either of the parents is in full employment there can be no help from the National Assistance Board although, if it were not for this rule, thousands of low-earning families would only too easily pass the means test.

This is a subject about which landlords are by no means alone in their lack of information. For who, not having studied it, would dream that families who are on national assistance are in very great numbers living *below* – and sometimes more than £2 a week below – the weekly rate which Parliament has fixed as the minimum for maintaining health?

Cut-Rate National Assistance

The people who would ordinarily be entitled to national assistance at the full rate all suffer from the same disability: they are unable to do full-time work and, usually, any work at all. This may be due to old age, illness, disablement, genuine unemployment, or to the fact that they have to stay at home to look after young children. These are the people who, whether or not they are getting pensions or insurance benefits, are poor enough to pass the official means test.

Among these there are two large groups of people, numbering together 56,000 (not counting wives or children), who although they qualify for full-scale assistance are not getting it – I am quoting the latest available figures – for reasons of pure expediency.

The first of these are low-earners who lose their jobs through no fault of their own; for instance, through redundancy or through a firm going bankrupt. If their family income on national assistance would be greater than when they were bringing home a wage, it must be cut down to *below* the level of that wage, no matter how low it was and no matter what poverty then existed. The cut can be anything up to £2 a week, and in some cases even more. This procedure is called the 'wage-stop'. It hits the biggest and poorest families hardest. Inevitably it is a cause of rent arrears and homelessness. In 1962, a year of heavy unemployment, particularly in the low-earning north and north-east, no less than 25,000 families were affected, and certainly not less than 125,000 men, women, and children.

Rent Allowances

What characterizes the second group of under-assisted people is that all of them are paying decontrolled rents.

Every national assistance allowance, although paid as one sum (in the form of a weekly money order cashable at a post office), contains two quite separate allowances. One is for necessities such as food and fuel and is based on scale rates (according to the age of the children, etc.) agreed by Parliament. The other is for rent. How then can it happen that a tenant who is not in the group described in the last paragraph, but who is on national assistance, may be quite unable to pay his rent?

The reason may be one of many. For instance, although this tenant is of course committed to paying his rent, he may also have committed himself, while earning a decent wage, to hire-purchase payments; or he may be obliged by law to pay maintenance for a wife or children from whom he is separated. In other words he can be faced with three choices: eviction for rent arrears, prison for debt, or just plain hunger. No doubt the landlord would hold that he has first claim, and with some reason. The tenant's rent allowance from the National Assistance Board is intended to be spent exclusively on rent. It can be withdrawn if it is spent on anything else but rent. All the same the choice, to put it mildly, is not an easy one.

In the great majority of cases this rent allowance is the exact amount of the rent charged, including rates. But it can be less – and less by anything from a few shillings to £2 a week, or even more – if the rent is considered to be 'unreasonable in the circumstances'. That does not mean that it is necessarily a high rent in actual money. For a rent of as little as £2 10s. a week can be judged unreasonable if charged for a very small and shoddy room in a heavily overcrowded house.

But the important point is that a tenant whose rent is considered unreasonable by the National Assistance Board is caught between cruel pincers. If he is to pay his rent he has somehow got to find the difference between what the landlord charges and what the Board allows. And how is he to do that except by taking it out of his allowance for bare necessities? In 1962 no less than 31,000 rent-payers found themselves in this appalling fix through no fault of their own, and again this figure excludes wives and children.

One of the worst aspects of this very great hardship (which affects people, old and young, paying rent of up to £7 a week – none were paying more) is that the victims usually do not in the least understand what has hit them, or even that they have been hit. All they know is that they are quite unable to make ends come anywhere near meeting. But they are not alone in their incomprehension. The mysteries of national assistance are, for instance, very seldom understood by solicitors. Almost invariably, they look on them as being quite outside their sphere.

For this reason landlords are very seldom told the real reason for rent arrears. Nor are the courts. And the result is that perfectly honest tenants can find themselves accused of fecklessness or – worse than that – find themselves evicted simply because the State has let them down; or, to put it another way, because the State has not felt it proper that public funds should go into the pockets of profiteering private landlords.

The figures quoted for these two groups of under-assisted people are to be found in what at the time of writing is the most recent report of the National Assistance Board, published in June 1963. See also pages 158–9.

What Can Be Done?

Every tenant on national assistance is entitled to ask what sum he is being allowed for rent or whether, for any other reason such as the wage-stop, he is getting less than full-scale assistance. He should ask for the figures and reasons to be written down for him. The Board does not normally do this except where there is to be an appeal to a tribunal. But there is no reason why it should not, and the information will be a great help to the tenant and his advisers.

The result of pointing out to the National Assistance Board that an under-assisted family or individual is in genuine hardship or in danger of eviction has often resulted in a deficient allowance being increased, sometimes up to the full amount.

If, however, the National Assistance Board decides that it cannot increase a rent allowance, the tenant can appeal (though without legal aid provision) to a National Assistance Board tribunal. If that does not help either – and he understandably does not care for the idea of appealing to a charity, or if a charity feels unable to subsidize an unreasonable rent – it is still just possible that the landlord may agree to take less rent until the tenant can go back to work and can then start paying off the difference. But that of course does not apply to old or disabled people.

As these 'unreasonable' rents always concern decontrolled and privately owned property, it is futile for a tenant with notice to quit to sit tight when it expires and let his landlord take him to court, because his hardship cannot be considered.

If the worst happens and the tenant becomes homeless it is obviously important that the welfare authorities should understand why he has got into arrears. Otherwise he could easily be taken for a deliberate defaulter. This can very seriously affect the kind of temporary accommodation he and his family will get and their chances, if any, of being rehoused.

It is only very recently that the State has seen fit to punish tenants for the sins of their landlords in this way, and to do so under the pretence of 'having regard to their welfare', which is one of its first duties under the National Assistance Act. Until creeping decontrol was introduced in 1957, the State did not often find itself driven to adopt such fantastic practices because the great majority of rents were controlled and the question of their being unreasonable did not therefore arise. But since then the smallest and lowest-rated homes, let unfurnished, have been becoming decontrolled at the rate of 300,000 a year, and the rents charged for them have pushed up those let furnished, so causing a continuous and upwards-spiralling trend, and one which is bound to become progressively more expensive. But in a rich country that is no justification.

The State's Point of View

What the State is saying to the tenant is roughly this:

'Although you, like every one else, are one of our members, we cannot help you at all to pay what we might agree is an unreasonable rent, as long as you are working. You should not be living where you are if you have such low wages and a wife who cannot go out to work because you have young children. And before going any further, we do not think it politic to provide enough day nurseries to solve that problem. We must not openly encourage mothers of young children to abandon their traditional role – unless of course they are unmarried – even though the whole economy of the country would be threatened if all of them stayed at home.

'On the other hand you must not try to solve your problem yourself by asking for higher wages – we take the poorest possible view of that. Nor must you leave your job before first finding another: we shall allow you less money than anyone else if you become what we call "voluntarily unemployed". But we are afraid that even if you become redundant in industry, we shall still have to punish you; because with your rent to meet (unreasonable or not), and all those children to cater for, your proper assistance allowance might come to £12 or £13 a week; and although we know that that is the minimum on which you can be expected to keep healthy and out of debt and of crime, we cannot let you have it because you did somehow manage on your own, when you were working, on only £10 or £11 – now didn't you?

'Surely you must see that if we did otherwise there would be a public outcry, because what we are using to supplement your national insurance unemployment benefit (on which, we agree, you cannot live and pay rent) is money contributed not by you, but by your richer fellow-citizens through income tax – which you were too poor to have to pay. And while we know that you cannot find another job (since you must of course be registered for employment to get our help at all), the public will take it that you are lolling about in luxury at its expense; and we do not, in the circumstances, feel it proper to tell it otherwise.

'We ourselves would dearly like to tell you that among your crimes is that of having children; but you might object rather strongly if you got the idea that this had become a right reserved for people who can earn more than you can. We have not yet reached the point where we would feel able to say that a man on £10 a week should not have more than three or four children or, indeed, any at all. Child-rationing has not yet been adopted, although in an overcrowded island it may come. Meanwhile this matter of excess infants is a rather delicate one from many aspects, not excluding that of religion. And there have been times, for instance during the war, when we held quite the opposite point of view.

'However, we do appreciate that you may not have sinned in this way at all. Perhaps before you became redundant or ill or bereaved or old, you had a decent income of, say, £16 a week or more; and perhaps you had no children, or only one or two, or they were not living with you. But even if this is so, and you did not succumb to our encouragement to involve yourself with hire purchase, or with private insurance, we still cannot help you at the proper rate because, in our view, you have not found yourself exactly the right kind of accommodation – neither above nor below what we see as your "requirements" – yet with a rent of not more than £3 10s. because that is as far as we think it reasonable to go.

'In refusing to go further, we hope no one will say that we would rather that your children went cold and hungry. We do lay ourselves open to that kind of jibe. And we hope particularly that it will not be assumed that we would rather that you became homeless, because that could cost the public twenty times more a week than it would to meet your rent. What you really should have done if you had any choice – and we know you had none – would have been to get yourself a council flat – though not, for preference, one in a new block, or one where a differential rent scheme operates, or one of those very expensive "mobiles" – as we prefer you, for purposes of assistance, to have a straightforward rent of under £2. Alternatively, if you were previously in rent-controlled property you should, whatever its condition and no matter what the property owners may say, have stayed in it. As it is, you have put us, as a welfare state, in a horribly embarrassing position.'

*

This, however, is not the only dilemma in which the State has found itself – as the next chapter will show. Nor is this the only circumstance in which it is trying to extricate itself at the expense of the tenant.

7 Landlords Under Compulsion

In the last few years the government has tried to put handcuffs and straitjackets on the most unruly private landlords, especially those found to be overcharging, overcrowding their houses, keeping them in a squalid condition, or failing to produce rent books or, in the case of property companies, their proper names.

In planning this campaign, little account seems to have been taken of certain very awkward obstacles. How, for instance, can overcrowding be dealt with under a housing shortage which is the cause of it? Who can say what overcharging means where rents are free from control? And if tenants have no security (and most concerned have none) what is to stop landlords from getting rid of them to save their own skins?

Rather obviously, the success of an action against an exploiting landlord depends on the tenant's still being under his roof and still being exploited when the case is heard. But because such cases have to be brought by local authorities, the chances are that they may never be heard at all.

Local authorities (who have lately been given greater powers to deal with wicked landlords and certain kinds of houses) cannot, by their very nature, start legal proceedings against them the moment an offence comes to light. Whole networks of proper channels must first be gone through. Reports must be made to senior officials. Decisions must be taken on whether a case is a proper one to go before a committee, which may meet only once in six weeks and already have an overweight agenda. And at every stage the alleged offence must be checked and re-checked to make sure that it still exists.

All this is inevitable. But frequent visits to a house are bound to put any landlord on his guard. (In fact, one landlord of an unimaginably gruesome house hastily lowered his rents after a single visit by a friend of one of the tenants who, for his own interest, took some photographs.) But most local authorities, as well as showing their hands by showing their faces, think it only right formally to warn landlords of probable action against them, often giving them several months' grace before going any further. And it is at this stage, if not earlier, that landlords are likely to clear their houses of tenants in order to escape retribution.

The landlords who can least easily take this evading action are those who own big tenement blocks (because they can hardly clear out a hundred or more tenants without causing a public scandal), and those with only one house in which they live themselves. But landlords who own more than one house are much better placed. And it is not unusual, nowadays, to meet families whose landlords have cleared them out of one house where there was a threat of council action and dumped them in another, repeating the process as necessary. In the course of a year or two, some families have been switched from house to house five or six times and have become so apathetic in the process that they no longer count themselves lucky not to be completely homeless.

Very often landlords have to act with great speed; and for this reason they sometimes prefer transferring tenants to giving them four weeks' notice to quit. Besides, the willingness of these tenants to pay high rents and to put up with squalor without complaint makes them valuable. But if there is nowhere else to put them, and if they do not get out when ordered to do so, they can find themselves forced out by other means.

In one house there were six immigrant families, all of whom had been met at the docks and taken there by a representative of a property company. This company was naturally assumed to be the owner. But, in fact, the house was owned by a convent in a northern city, and the mother superior had not given her permission for it to be used for letting. Previously it had been used for storage, and it was fit for nothing else. This company was a small-scale affair formed by a disreputable estate agent. Exactly what he was up to or how he got hold of the property was never known. But the suggestion was that he had been embezzling the rents he charged to the tune of £3 per room, or £18 a week. This might have gone on undetected if the local health authority had not heard that the house was packed to overflowing. Counting the children, there were about thirty-five people in it. The instant after the inspector called, the agent – in an understandable panic – began operations to force the tenants out. And in spite of the fact that all the children were very young, and some of them infants, he cut off the gas and water and electricity. Some landlords, however, go even further than that and remove doors and windows and have w.c.s padlocked. Where there is a will there is always a way – and one short of physical violence – to clear a house. And although the tenants will afterwards be able to sue the landlord, if they know their rights and have not entirely lost faith in the law's protection, the local authority can find itself neatly baulked.

None of this is at all well known, probably because no local authority likes to admit that a landlord has got the better of it, or that a tenant has suffered as a result of its intervention. But even if there were more publicity about the dangers of attempting to use compulsion on individual landlords, it could still be argued that they must be dealt with and that the effect must be that some tenants, at any rate, will afterwards enjoy better conditions.

So they will, and in large numbers. But for reasons which will soon become obvious these favoured tenants are, more often than not, single people who could quite easily get better accommodation on their own initiative. And, just as ironically, the landlords who find themselves charged with overcrowding their houses are often the least deserving of punishment. For these are the landlords, usually coloured people, who do not bar children and who, whether consciously or not, are keeping thousands of them out of institutions for the homeless.

These are only a few of the ill-effects of this hastily devised and largely unworkable system. New powers of compulsion will of course help. For, armed with these, a local authority will be able to pounce on any house in multiple occupation where the tenants' 'safety, health, and welfare' appear to be endangered, and will be able to take it over, without any of the usual time-wasting preliminaries, for a maximum of five years.

This is exactly the sort of treatment that the real bad-hats among private landlords deserve and have invited; and the very fear of it may act as a powerful curb. But not many local authorities may relish having to hand back to such landlords houses which they have put in order or tenants whose safety they have restored. And this pouncing action is expected to be taken only as a last resort when present methods have already failed. So the worst landlords are likely, as now, to extricate themselves before there is any real danger of losing control of their houses, of being compelled to carry out expensive repair operations, or of finding themselves deprived of their incomes from rents. Many of them will simply force out their tenants, as now, and sell with vacant possession. But other methods of evasion have already appeared. As soon as the take-over proposals were published, some landlords began to thin out their tenants, keeping only those who could pay higher rents and giving them extra rooms.

Another reason why pouncing is likely to be infrequent is that there will be no compulsion or duty to practise it. And to do so without first investigating conditions could land a local authority in court, because the pouncee will have a right of appeal. Besides the whole undertaking is a heavier one than most local authorities – already overworked and understaffed – will shoulder with any eagerness. And their position as temporary landlords is bound to be embarrassing in so many ways that this alone may prove a powerful deterrent. Some of these embarrassments, especially those affecting tenants, will be discussed later in this chapter. But it will necessarily deal chiefly with forms of compulsion that are already in use.

DISCOVERING THE LANDLORD'S NAME

The tenant who pays his rent weekly and whose landlord is a property company has had, since 1962, a right to ask for the names of all the members of the company's board (and that of its secretary), and local authorities can prosecute if this information is withheld. As it is a simple matter for anyone to find out the name of the chairman and secretary of any company from the Companies' Register, the intended effect of taking this action was apparently that of alerting offending property companies to the danger of public exposure by their tenants.

One difficulty here, as with so many other rights, is that only the tenant with security of tenure can safely take action. Another is that property companies can very conveniently switch the ownership of their houses to another company in the same group, in order to avoid prosecution. At the time of writing not a single case of successful action has been publicly reported.

EXCESSIVE RENTS

The need to do something about excessive rents was obvious long before the Rent Act was passed. Rent tribunals had been trying to deal with them in furnished accommodation since 1946. But it was not until four years after decontrol – whether of the creeping or the instant variety – had hit unfurnished accommodation that a need to help stricken tenants was recognized.

For some quite incomprehensible reason it had previously been thought that the tenant of decontrolled property, although without a single trump up his sleeve, would find himself in a fair position to bargain with his landlord about the rent he should pay. And in the government's handbook *The Rent Act and You*, published in 1957, Question 9 and its answer ran as follows:

What rent is payable under a new tenancy?
That is for the tenant to agree with the landlord, and must depend on the value of the house. If either of them is in doubt about the current rental value of the house, he should get professional advice.

But no one told the unfortunate professional advisers what to advise. Nor would that have been possible, because a decontrolled house has no 'current rental value' in actual figures. What the advisers found themselves obliged to say to prospective tenants was this:

Can you pay what the landlord is asking? If not, someone else probably will – even if the landlord has to wait a bit to get his price.

Fair bargaining between landlords and tenants is obviously possible only where housing supply and demand are almost equal. Otherwise the landlord who, as the owner, always holds not only the ace of trumps, but the whole pack, is in a position to raise his stakes according to the local height of the housing shortage.

The proportion of income which people should, ideally, pay for housing is – according to most experts – not more than one fifth. But countless families have been obliged to pay more than 50 per cent of earnings in order to escape being homeless. And in one case, the parents of two small children were found to be paying £7 a week for two rooms in a shoddy district, out of total earnings of only £8 a week. As the National Assistance Board cannot help where either parent is in full-time work, this family – like many others – could avoid starvation only by borrowing from friends.

COMPULSORY PURCHASE

Compulsory purchase was to be the weapon used against overcharging. But when local authorities were invited by the government to use their powers, they were plunged into difficulties, other than financial, which are little known.

In the first place, compulsory purchase powers could not be used merely if tenants were paying exorbitant rents. They had to be 'in danger of becoming homeless under the threat of exorbitant rents'. And the Minister of Housing himself did not find it easy to define what an exorbitant rent is. He put it this way:

> Rents of particular properties cannot necessarily be said to be reasonable merely because some tenants are prepared to pay them, any more than they can necessarily be said to be exorbitant simply because some tenants refuse to pay them.

This made it more than a little hard for local authorities to know which properties would be considered suitable by the Minister for compulsory buying, and which would not. The result, in 1962, was that thirteen cases were rejected and ten withdrawn. And the number of orders which were confirmed by the Minister was precisely four.

But there are quite other reasons why local authorities submit so very few proposals to the Minister. The most flagrant cases of overcharging, in relation to rateable values and state of repair, occur in single houses and not in tenement blocks – on which a few orders have been made. An obvious reason for this is that in tenement blocks tenants often form their own powerful associations with the result that landlords fear exposure if they overcharge too heavily. In single houses there is much less risk, and less still if the tenants are coloured people, because they will be the least likely to dare to complain.

In one case a coloured family was paying a rent which made even the local council gasp: £9 10s. a week for an East London four-room terrace house, without a bathroom and in a hopeless state of disrepair. But an appeal for a compulsory purchase order was turned down by the council because the effect would have been that a newcomer to this country would have gained all the advantages of being a council tenant. His rent would have been reduced, the repairs to the house done, and a bathroom and other improvements put into it. Local families waiting year after year for a council house would feel, it was feared, great resentment and bitterness – and so would the ratepayers generally.

Some of the most shameless overcharging occurs also in subdivided houses where as many tenants as possible are crammed into the smallest possible space. But here a council which, through compulsory purchase, became the actual and permanent owner would have to reduce overcrowding and rehouse the surplus tenants – again over the heads of waiting-list families. In a house where all the rooms were let to nurses from a certain hospital the rent for each room was until recently £5 a week. Then the landlord announced that the rooms would be cut in two by partitions and that the rent of each half would be £4 10s. How could a local council be expected to step in and rehouse all the tenants? They would need bed-sitting rooms of the type used for rehousing old people, and of which there has long been a tragic shortage. Also in uncontrolled property tenants can be evicted before the Minister has agreed to a compulsory purchase order.

COMPULSORY IMPROVEMENTS

The rate at which landlords have been repairing their houses with the help of grants has been so disappointing that compulsion first came under consideration in 1962.

Stanley Alderson puts the situation very neatly when he says in his Penguin book *Housing*:

About 26,000 baths a year are being installed in private property.

At this rate it will take a century and a quarter to equip more than 3 million privately rented houses that now have either no bath or a shared one.

But not by any means all houses have a backyard where a bathroom and W.C. for even one family could be built. And tenants can hardly be expected to give up a room to get a little more convenience, only to find themselves very inconveniently overcrowded. There is also the very discouraging prospect of having to pay extra rates plus a considerable amount of extra rent. For a landlord can increase a controlled rent by $12\frac{1}{2}$ per cent of what the improvements cost him, and this will be a continuing charge to the tenant year after year.

Landlords, on the other hand, naturally jib at putting in improvements voluntarily because they are afterwards obliged, as a condition of getting a grant, to keep their houses open for letting and to charge controlled rents. Until now this frustrating period has been ten years – on the higher 'discretionary' grants.

Under the latest scheme, landlords can be compelled to put in improvements; the period of control is to be very much shortened; the rents chargeable (in decontrolled property) are to be very much increased; and, in certain cases, there will be no compulsion to put in all five standard improvements: bath, W.C., fixed basin, larder, and hot-water system. Also, a bath need not be put into a room of its own, and a shower can very sensibly be substituted – though where either are to go if not into a bathroom has yet to be explained.

Everyone wants to see the disappearance of the tin bath in the kitchen, the far-flung W.C., the tap in the yard, the gas cooker used to store food. Any advance towards that end is a welcome one, as long as it does not seriously reduce the amount of available living space or lead to the displacement of families from decontrolled property. And although some tenants will certainly find themselves under pressure from their landlords to object to the improvement of their homes (because no compulsion can be used on a landlord for ten years if the tenant objects for all that time), at least this could act as a rather curious form of protection against eviction.

DEALING WITH SQUALOR AND OVERCROWDING

One of the most fantastic results of the housing shortage is that, nowadays, there can be a need to defend tenants against efforts on the part of health authorities to compel their landlords to improve their living conditions.

The houses concerned are officially known as 'houses-let-in-lodgings' or houses 'in multiple occupation'. In nearly all cases they are Victorian and were originally designed for the use of only one family; and they are found in once-prosperous but now seedy parts of cities. Most of them are structurally sound and so are not yet due for clearance, although internally they can be slums of unimaginable squalor. Liverpool has some particularly ripe specimens.

So great is the need for housing among people of low income that it has been found very easy, and profitable, to let each room or pair of rooms separately, either to families or to adults renting singly or in groups. Far too many people, sometimes thirty or more, have to share a single W.C., and there is rarely a bathroom, a hot-water system, or any place to store perishable food. Cookers are often placed on landings or inside rooms where families live and sleep in company with slop-buckets. There may be only a couple of dustbins, permanently overflowing. The last thing one can expect to find is a fire escape. Tenants come and go – often into, and out of, accommodation for the homeless – at an alarming pace. Despair and poverty (for the rents are usually not less than £2 10s. per week for each room) lead to the kind of apathy which results in the passages, stairs, and landings being left uncleaned. Often washing has to be hung on a line over a coal fire in a room where the windows have long ago refused to open, and where every inch of space is taken up by beds and cots whose mattresses can never be aired.

One man, asked what sort of room he had got for his rent of £3 10s. a week, replied, 'I have not got a room – I have got a cage. There is not even room for a chair. In our house we all have to live like animals. It is a human zoo.'

Another man found himself and his wife and two babies in an all-purpose room about 10 ft by 6 ft where the decaying walls were smeared with squashed bugs. The house was chiefly used by prostitutes, and there were frequent brawls at night. The family had been dumped there as a result of local authority action against their landlord for failing to provide tolerable living conditions in the house in which they previously lived. This action had been taken under the Housing Act of 1961.

POWERS OF THE HOUSING ACT 1961

Part 2 of this Act empowered public health authorities to require landlords to put their overcrowded houses in order and to supply proper sanitary facilities. But landlords can get round the obligation to spend money on extra w.c.s and other necessities for civilized living if they can show that they have suitably reduced the number of people using those facilities which already exist. This, of course, means evicting surplus tenants. So does a directive by the health authorities to reduce numbers to a certain maximum. Very often this maximum is five because that is thought to be a tolerable number of people to one w.c.

Unfortunately, local authorities have no power to direct landlords as to how they should reduce the 'number of persons' in any house, nor do they hold themselves responsible for the subsequent evictions. In fact some hold that landlords are only required to limit numbers after the present tenants have left. But when asked if notices to quit already issued can therefore be withdrawn, a usual reply is that that would be 'quite contrary to the council's intentions'.

Under other legislation dealing with overcrowding (i.e. the ratio of people to space and the number of people *sleeping* in any given room) children from the age of one to ten count only as half 'persons', and babies not yet a year old do not officially exist at all. But under the Housing Act 1961 children of any age count as full persons. And, because of this, families are in much greater danger of eviction than childless adults.

COMPULSION AS A CAUSE OF HOMELESSNESS

In a certain house, for instance, there were seventeen people and the health authorities required a reduction by five. The landlord, not unnaturally, chose to evict a family of five (mother, father, and three small children) because by so doing he lost only one rent. For all the other twelve people in the house were adults – some living alone, some in pairs – and to achieve the required reduction he would have had to evict four tenants instead of one, with a consequent loss of £10 a week in rent instead of only £2 15s. The evicted family became homeless and was split up, the mother and children going to a reception centre where conditions were a great deal more insanitary and overcrowded than those they had endured at home.

This happened in London where the authority to take this public-health action is the borough council and the authority responsible for sheltering the homeless is the county council. Research is likely to show that the mounting numbers of London's homeless families are partially due to this cause. In one London borough, fifty houses had been dealt with in this way by October 1963; and, in case after case, the victims were exclusively parents and children.

PROVIDING OTHER ACCOMMODATION

Sometimes, when protests are made to local authorities that they are causing homelessness, they urge landlords to find other accommodation for the surplus families they have to evict. But often the landlords of these houses are coloured newcomers who own only one house which they had to buy to avoid becoming homeless themselves. Obviously they cannot help. Others who can, and who want to keep on the right side of the council, sometimes find accommodation for a surplus family simply by evicting another from a house elsewhere. And, to make things worse, health authorities have no duty to inspect the new accommodation. That is how a family can find itself in a bug-ridden room and in a house used for prostitution through public health action.

NEW COMPULSIONS, NEW DANGERS

If local authorities make use of new compulsory powers to take over certain of the most disgracefully run houses in multiple occupation, they will become the temporary landlords. As they will also take over the duty of reducing the number of people in these houses, they will find themselves in the very embarrassing position of having to evict at least some of their own newly acquired tenants, without being able to charge them with any offence but simply because for health reasons they are redundant.

Unlike private landlords, local authorities will not have to calculate – in choosing whom to evict – what will be the most financially profitable solution in the matter of rents. And obviously they will not pick on families with children where there is any choice. But in many of these teeming houses there may, in fact, be no choice. For, so often, every room or pair of rooms contains parents and children; and it can also happen that the presence of one big family is the sole cause of excessive numbers.

This is so, at the moment, in a house containing six rooms, two of them in the basement, and each pair let separately. The top floor pair is let to an elderly and disabled married couple; the two below are occupied by their six grandchildren and their parents; the basement is rented by a single man. How would a local authority, deciding that eleven people were too many for the use of one w.c., handle this situation if it became the temporary landlord? Presumably it would do exactly what it recently required the owner to do: reduce numbers from eleven to five with the consequent necessity of giving notice to quit to the family with its six children, and with the eventual effect of relieving congestion for the sole benefit of childless people. In this case an additional effect will be that of leaving two old people without the family support which they so much need themselves and which they in their turn also give by letting two of their grandchildren sleep in their part of the house – and by minding them generally.

Another purpose of these take-overs will be to compel recalcitrant landlords to carry out repairs. And where that is not a practical possibility, the local authority can carry out the repairs itself and recover the cost from the property – which is thought to mean by collecting the rents. But in many cases the repairs and improvements needed are likely to be so extensive and thoroughgoing that all the tenants will have to be given notice to quit. And if any of them are protected tenants with security of tenure, they will find, in these circumstances, that this protection is meaningless. Even now, a private landlord can get a so-called protected tenant out, via a court order, if his presence prevents the carrying out of a local authority directive. One man, with a family, whose tenancy was protected under the Rent Act, was encouraged to let his case go to court so that this injustice in the law could be seen to exist. But his landlord became violent and his wife was so terrified that she preferred to go with her new-born baby and two other small children into a reception centre for homeless families. Meanwhile, the father slept out for several nights until he could find a bed in a doss-house.

So far, no duty has been placed on local authorities to rehouse newly taken-over tenants whom they themselves may have to evict. Indeed, if they were given this duty, the whole system would become unworkable because they would certainly feel unable to give such tenants priority over families on their waiting lists. Ironically enough, many of these families who have been waiting year after year for a reprieve are much more painfully overcrowded, but do not happen to live in the type of house where local authority take-overs can be made. The criterion here is not the amount of living space occupied by any one family, but the number of separate households, and the total number of people, in any one privately owned house. In fact, if this were not so, many local authorities would find themselves unable to turn a blind eye on overcrowding in their own properties.

Already there is very great and understandable disillusion-ment among families made homeless by private landlords under pressure from local public health authorities. But when those authorities become themselves responsible for evicting blameless tenants, that disillusionment is likely to deepen into bitterness; and no one can predict how deep, especially in young people, it will go – unless other homes are found for them, perhaps by buying old houses on the open market or by compulsory pur-chase.

One of the cruellest and least understood aspects of this problem is that the families now living in these subdivided houses have frequently had even less choice in the matter than might be supposed. The reason here is that they were previously in an institution for the homeless. For when families are in this pitiful condition, pressure is put on them by the welfare authorities sheltering them to 'find their own accommodation'; and if they are known to have found but refused this – perhaps on the grounds that they would be hopelessly overcrowded or that the place is unbearably squalid in every sort of way – they can be turned out as being uncooperative. In fact, it has frequently happened that welfare authorities – overwhelmed by mounting numbers – have themselves found and induced families to take rooms in just the type of house which is now under public health action.

WHAT IT MEANS TO BE HOMELESS

In answer to charges of causing homelessness, local authorities in London – and private landlords too – are beginning to suggest that to be homeless is no longer such a disaster as it was only a year or two ago.

Certainly, homeless families in L.C.C. London are now being rehoused, usually in old and substandard council property, at a much accelerated pace. Occasionally the interval is as short as four months. Unhappily, however, these rescue operations are being achieved very largely at the expense of overcrowded families on the waiting list whose adolescent sons and daughters often have to share rooms, if not beds, or are packed into one room with their parents. Even those with special priority or urgent medical grounds have to wait for a reprieve – not for months, but for years. The new 'mobile' housing in the form of very small prefabricated bungalows – known as 'biscuit tins' – is available only to families of suitable size and able to pay more than £4 p.w.

But while homelessness in L.C.C. London can be a short-cut to a council flat, it is usually anything but a painless one. Because there is still only one L.C.C. reception centre where whole homeless families can be together in decent conditions (it opened in 1962 and is the only one of its kind in the whole country), and because it can take only eighty families, the great majority of mothers and children still have to go into old and insalubrious workhouse accommodation – initially at any rate.

In the worst centre of this kind there is a total lack of privacy, gross overcrowding, inadequate sanitation, and no place for isolating ill children. Although both mothers and children are swabbed (rectally) on admission, infections and illnesses, particularly dysentery, rage. Hardly a day passes without the arrival of an ambulance and the removal of children to hospital. And if a mother is for this reason left without any of her children, she has to leave the centre and find herself temporary lodgings until the children come back – often to be infected again.

This is part of the terrible price that far too often has to be paid for homelessness. It is feared even more than the separation of husbands and wives, the scattering of children who are too old to go into a centre with their mothers yet too young either to be left on their own or, if they are boys, to go into lodging houses with their fathers. It is feared much more than the destitution which these separations so often cause. Cheerless and squalid conditions and poor food – for which high charges are nevertheless made* – are as nothing in comparison. Sometimes the fear of illness leads to mothers abandoning their children while they are in hospital because at least they are safe there. For owing to the shortage of hospital beds children have to be discharged the moment they are well enough, even though the hospital authorities are fully aware that the parents have nowhere to take them. Often, homeless parents refuse to risk their children's health – especially if they are very young – by taking them into a reception centre in the first place. They try, instead, to have them put straight into a children's home, or to have them placed with strangers who will be their foster parents. But as this alternative solution is frowned on officially, they have to struggle, and sometimes to threaten desertion, to achieve it.

In some cases these children become permanently separated from their parents, if they cannot afterwards find a home where they will be admitted; and they are rarely visited, because this only means another unbearable separation after a few hours. Very often such parents also have to bear criticism from the authorities on the grounds that in failing to visit they are being callous.

* In Newington Lodge where a mother and two children may have to sleep in a dormitory the charge is £5 p.w. In the L.C.C.'s best centre at Hackney each family has one room and charges are from £7 p.w.

One young couple who did get their children back, by paying £5 a week for one room and a kitchen in a house in multiple occupation, are now faced with homelessness again because of local authority action to reduce numbers. The mother formerly left a reception centre because her baby was put into a cot from which an infected child had just been removed to hospital. Rather than go back she has said that she would gas herself and the children.

But outside L.C.C. London the price of homelessness can be, in some respects, even stiffer. No official research has been done into conditions, and the only way of finding out anything about them is by means of personal investigation.

Old workhouse buildings are still used for homeless mothers and children almost everywhere. Bare floorboards, iron bedsteads, hard chairs, insufficient bathrooms and w.c.s are usual. In a few places nissen huts, made relatively warm and comfortable, are substituted. In others big houses, unsuitable and unconverted for the purpose, are used as hostels and as many mothers and children as possible are crammed into the rooms without even the privacy of cubicles. Outbreaks of dysentery are by no means confined to central London.

In some workhouse buildings, mothers and children find themselves in what were the wash-houses and which have changed very little. In others they are lodged in the same wing as the casual wards for tramps. Where there are no small rooms, the accommodation can be so overcrowded that incoming mothers are told that they may have to sleep on a couple of chairs or on the floor. Where a county council, and not a county borough, is the authority responsible (under the National Assistance Act of 1948) for sheltering the homeless, mothers and children can find themselves stranded fifty miles or so from home. On the other hand, there are some places where, because there is no severe shortage of council housing, evicted families are either rehoused straight away or put into specially reserved houses until there is a vacancy. Whether a family is broken up and remains so depends entirely on where it loses its home.

One of the cruellest practices outside the L.C.C. area – and often only just over the boundary line – is to accept homeless families in temporary accommodation but to limit their stay there to three months. At the end of that time notice to quit is served; and when that expires, eviction – if necessary by the police – follows. So, in most cases, does the separation of parents and children.

Without any doubt the L.C.C. is ahead of other authorities in making strenuous, if belated, efforts to make homelessness less intolerable, and either to keep families together or to reunite them as soon as possible. For this purpose it has recently provided much more second-stage family accommodation. But as well as being overwhelmed by unexpected numbers (otherwise its worst reception centre would long ago have been closed), it is also the most put-upon authority in the country. London draws people to it from every other part of the country (particularly from areas of unemployment) as well as from abroad. The fact that borough councils are not responsible for sheltering families displaced as a result of their action from overcrowded houses means an additional burden for the L.C.C. And there are some other county councils and county boroughs who, lacking space for their own homeless families, encourage them to try their luck in London and even pay their fares to go there. This, however, is a snare, because families who cannot prove that they are Londoners by residence are immediately sent back again; or if they refuse, their children are put into public care.

There are other unpublicized difficulties. For instance, mothers who normally go out to work can seldom do so while in reception centres, even if long journeys are not involved, because there are no playrooms for the children and no staff to look after them. The latter is also a severe handicap where mothers are under a threat of eviction from homeless accommodation if they do not search for vacant rooms. But, this apart, most landlords and landladies (other than coloured) are unwilling to consider prospective tenants whose present address is a reception centre because of the stigma which still attaches to being homeless and its built-in assumption that the cause must be rent arrears.

Many people who see advertisements in the press of vacant flats or rooms at not very steep rents naturally assume that homeless parents have not tried as hard as they might to help themselves. But this is to forget that, apart from the ban on children, private landlords – in the more desirable neighbourhoods where these vacancies usually occur – are also sharply selective on a class, job, speech, and appearance basis.

This situation was quite bad enough before the introduction of compulsory tenant-rationing. For homeless children and their parents, that can only mean more shut doors.

EXCESSIVE RENTS AND NATIONAL ASSISTANCE

Between this practice of tenant-rationing and that of the National Assistance Board in limiting rent allowances, there is a close connexion. They are compromise solutions to the twin problems of overcrowding and overcharging in privately rented property. What perhaps is not obvious is that a certain group of tenants stand to be hardest hit by both.

These tenants are newcomers to what they still call the mother country: they are people, chiefly coloured, from Commonwealth countries (particularly those most neglected by this one), whose services are badly needed here for all sorts of ill-paid and un-pleasant jobs, as well as on public transport, in hospitals and other public institutions, such as old people's homes, and in schools.

Where there is really gross overcrowding – and in one London house the police recently found forty-seven children – the tenants are almost always immigrants who detest living in such conditions but can find nothing better. The same is true where rents are most monstrous because coloured people are subjected to a blackness tax by private landlords and are increasingly pre-ferred as being more easily fleeceable than any others.

As the National Assistance Board does not grant more than £3 10s. (and frequently less) towards an unreasonable rent when tenants are unable to work – perhaps through illness or through having to stay at home to look after young children – the difference which somehow has to be found between that and the actual rent charged is usually greater for coloured tenants than for any others. As rents for grossly overcrowded conditions can, however low in terms of cash, also be judged unreasonable by the N.A.B., coloured people are affected to an extent out of all proportion to their numbers in this country. Out of the

31,000 rent-payers on national assistance in 1962 who did not, in the normal way, get their rents met in full, over one third, we are officially told, 'were immigrants from Commonwealth countries'. What all this means is that they are the most heavily penalized for the sins of their landlords or their own helplessness, and most in danger of being either starved out or pushed out of their homes by the indirect action of the State.

But the problem of what to do with homeless families in general has driven the State still further up an already excessively tall gum tree. Private landlordism has not only disrupted, and corrupted, our system of public welfare for people in their own homes – a system which for all its faults was previously one of the finest in the world – but has continued to do this after they are pushed out. Because private landlordism produces a vast amount of moribund housing totally unfit to live in, accommodation for the homeless never has been – and under this system never will be – adequate in either quantity or quality. For reasons of pure expediency and to prevent thousands of ill-housed people from deliberately making themselves homeless, it is deliberately made sufficiently wretched to deter. Yet its very wretchedness disgraces not only those directly responsible but the whole country in which it exists.

Recently a homeless mother described in a broadcast her arrival at a notorious reception centre. 'We got there about 7 o'clock ... I was shown the room where we had to sleep ... just one huge room with lots of families in it. And we just cried and we didn't know what to do. We were bewildered and the children kept crying for their Daddy. My little girl, she's been ill ever since it happened ... it has a general effect on all the children. I mean ... it's like a fright, a fear of being parted.'

And the father of a homeless family, a milkman, said this: 'The way things are going, you can't get a flat anywhere, with a wife and three children ... you just don't stand a chance, the young people of today, under at least £5 a week. I look in the papers, look on the boards, ask everywhere ... but the rents are too fantastic. You can take them but you find yourself in debt. A home life is a very great thing – it's something that should be treasured; you've got a home and a street door, you shut it and you say "I'm home, I'm with my family".'

8 Comments, Forecasts, and Suggestions

Behind countless doors and windows, particularly in the southeast, people are being driven to despair by having too little living space, from inability to pay high rents, from constant fear of eviction. Bewilderment that all this should be allowed in a civilized and rich country is turning into bitterness. Racial tensions which would be negligible but for competition are inevitably tightening. Seen at close quarters this is an explosive situation which threatens, if not taken quickly and resolutely in hand, to spill over into real social chaos.

Most people know the causes. It was not foreseen when postwar housing plans were made that we should have a rising birth rate; that young people would mature and marry earlier and would no longer meekly accept having to live with their relatives; that old people would live longer; and that people from all over the world would congregate here because of difficulties in their own countries. It would be easy but tedious to go on and on about declining industries in the north and about the monstrous burgeoning of office employment and building in the south; about land prices spiralling skywards, and council building, which alone caters on any considerable scale for the poor, languishing for lack of adequate financial support. Some of these causes suggest their own remedies; but none of them will be quick or painless, let alone complete. And meanwhile the need for first aid for the casualties – especially those unable to pay market prices to get themselves housed – grows daily more pressing.

The government is certainly not unaware of the seriousness of this need. But it has itself made the situation infinitely worse by the decontrol provisions of the Rent Act – the effect of which was rather like that of removing the safety valve from a vast pressure cooker. The dangers of bestowing powers on property owners which they had not enjoyed for nearly forty years were, it is true, foreseen – at least to the extent that, when introducing the Rent Act, the hope was expressed that landlords would behave with restraint. But that hope was so quickly dashed that only a year later the Landlord and Tenant Act of 1958 became necessary – and, after that, the Housing Act of 1961, and, after that, the Landlord and Tenant Act of 1962, all of which had the purpose of curbing the greed and checking the negligence of landlords, and of giving tenants certain defensive rights.

The chief reason why all these measures have failed is that defensive rights are as good as useless if tenants have only four weeks' security of tenure. Almost everything that has been done since 1957 to try to curtail suffering and injustice amounts to no more than tinkering with machinery which never could have worked. And the fact that the public has been encouraged to believe that it could shows a startling degree of cynicism on the part of the manufacturers.

THE CASE FOR PUBLIC OWNERSHIP

Inevitably, property owners have a vested interest in housing shortage. But whether they can exploit it or not is a matter for government. The blame for present malpractices does not therefore rest solely with the landlords. It was absurd and unfair to expect them not to use the great powers over their tenants which were bestowed upon them by the Rent Act. Theirs is a business, its aim is profit, and no business can be run in that way. A property company can hardly tell its shareholders that it has not even tried to get the maximum obtainable return on their investments.

But this raises the question of whether the ownership of other people's houses ought to be run as a business for private profit – especially now that so many small owners are being swallowed up by property companies which, by their very anonymity, can so much more easily evade their responsibilities. In one London borough, which has some of the most scabrous of slums to be found anywhere in the country, no less than eighty property companies are now operating; and that is not the maximum figure because, where tenants pay rates direct to the local authority, even the cover-name of the owner may be quite unknown.

The right of private landlords to continue to operate the letting market, although on a much reduced scale, has never seriously been challenged. But if it were, they would no doubt base their claim to continue partly on tradition, partly on the importance of private enterprise, and chiefly on the fact that they provide a very useful service. The best landlords do exactly that. But even at its best, theirs has never been, and never can be, a public service. And when, recently, the chairman of the National Federation of Property Owners maintained that private landlords do, in fact, provide a public service – and that this ought to be much more gratefully acknowledged by government and public alike – the occasion was not an altogether happy one: he had just suffered a compulsory purchase order on twenty of his East London blocks of flats because the rents charged had been found excessive and repairs had not been done.

The only feasible alternative – considering the very limited scale on which voluntary and non-profit-making housing societies can operate – is that local authorities should gradually take over. But because of violent adverse propaganda from people and organizations with property interests, what this would mean has been badly misrepresented. That we should become 'a nation of council tenants' is an idea which should positively commend itself to tenants of wicked landlords. But it is bound to sound grim to people living comfortably in their own houses, especially if they imagine that they would necessarily be taken over – which is not so – or do not realize that even if they were their most probable position would be that of occupying leaseholders for the lifetime of their houses. And not all owner-occupiers by any means would look with horror at the loss of freedom that losing their freeholds would entail. Because of the shortage of rentable houses and because of the fear of insecurity, thousands of people have been obliged to buy against their will and beyond their means. These include many elderly people who were formerly sitting tenants. And for them – as for all except the richest owners – upkeep and repairs are a constant financial nightmare. Assistance from local authorities is desperately needed to prevent houses, let alone their owners, from becoming prematurely unfit; and this could reasonably be expected if local authorities became the landlords.

But in any case the man who buys a freehold house no longer has the delightful assurance of peaceful and permanent security which was his chief object in buying it. If he lives in a small country town he may suddenly hear that it is to be expanded to twice its size and that factories are to sprout on its edges. If he lives in a village he may wake up to find an airport or a power station at the bottom of his garden. Even if his house is isolated in unspoilt country he can find his precious view entirely wrecked by a motorway (if, indeed, it does not come ploughing through his drawing-room). But in cities the owner-occupier is progressively more likely to find a compulsory purchase order on his breakfast table as the needs of private motorists – of whom he may well be one – become paramount, and as large decaying areas have to be rebuilt. In other words he is going to have less and less freedom to lose whether his legal status is changed or not. And looking at this from a rather less personal point of view, there are great disadvantages in big-scale owner-occupation. It delays interminably all improvement plans and it is one of the strongest deterrents against people moving, and therefore against industry moving too, away from suffocating cities.

All this apart, it is most unlikely that a take-over by local authorities if it ever happened would at first include anything at all but rented houses below a certain rateable value. So the freedom of the owner-occupier, such as it is, would be temporarily quite unaffected; and the freedom of the rich to go on renting from private landlords at exorbitant prices would also be preserved.

But, significantly, the rich themselves are increasingly anxious for their rented homes to be taken over by local authorities, as requests for compulsory purchase action on blocks of London luxury flats has lately shown. And the old idea, so strenuously put about, that to 'live under the council' means all kinds of pettifogging restrictions on personal liberty is rapidly losing ground.

In fact, such restrictions are scarcely ever unreasonable and are usually made with the sole purpose of safeguarding other tenants. And they are trivial in comparison with those so often imposed by private landlords. No council tenant ever gets notice to quit because his wife is expecting a baby.

What perhaps is feared most is that under a system of public ownership of rented houses there would be much less freedom to choose where to live. But council tenants are free to apply for transfers, and they move about with surprising frequency. They can also arrange their own exchanges, as long as they can get approval for what they propose. And this approval is withheld only if either family would as a result have too few rooms or too many.

That raises another very important point. One of the great disadvantages of private landlordism is that it is not concerned with using existing living space to the best advantage, from a human or social point of view; and that in turn was one of the reasons why the Rent Act was bound to fail in its aims of curing overcrowding and under-occupation. The average private landlord does not worry if a single tenant has one all-purpose room for his family, or six unoccupied rooms, as long as he pays the rent.

Admittedly, local authorities do not always make the fullest possible use of their houses and flats either. But they do make the most strenuous efforts to fit their in-coming tenants into the most economical amount of space. The only reason why they do not later oblige them to move, when children leave home and leave spare rooms, is that the last thing they want is to make their tenants feel insecure or under bureaucratic compulsion. On the other hand tenants with more space than they need can ask for, or be offered, something smaller; and reasonable requests to take in lodgers are not refused, as they so very often are, lawfully or not, by private landlords.

To anyone who has for years observed, without prejudice, the position of tenants of local authorities, their advantages over those of private landlords look from every angle tremendous. Their accommodation has to be of a good standard; and old houses now being bought for waiting-list families, though not for homeless families, for example by the London County Council, are usually splendidly improved and decorated and fitted with modern kitchens, bathrooms, w.c.s, hot-water systems, and so on, before occupation; their rents are never unreasonable and can be varied according to income; urgent repairs are seldom neglected for long; and only the damage done by tenants them- selves is their own liability. But their greatest advantage is that they are in no fear of trickery or intimidation or exploitation be- cause their landlords are responsible public bodies. What these tenants chiefly lack is some means of appeal against the occa- sionally harsh and unfair decisions of those bodies. The best remedy would be the appointment of a special commissioner with full powers to look into grievances about bad administration – on the model of the Scandinavian Ombudsman. At the very least there should be a right of appeal to the courts or to independent tribunals. At the moment these harsh decisions chiefly concern evictions for small arrears of rent incurred through circumstances beyond the tenants' control. But too great bureaucratic power is always dangerous and the insolence of office is a very dreadful thing.

Although local authorities are constantly buying private pro- perty in order to pull it down, or buying it – on a much smaller but increasing scale – to put their own tenants into it, the possi- bility of a general take-over of the lower-rated rented houses is still pretty remote. It is no longer part of official Labour Party policy, for undisclosed reasons. So, for the moment at any rate, one has to look at other possible ways of checking the present excesses of the worst private landlords.

THE LANDLORDS' ANSWER

What do the landlords' associations, in their own interests, pro- pose? The answer is fascinating because it is so devious. In a statement published in the *Observer*, and no doubt in many other newspapers, on 15 September 1963, a representative of the property owners' new joint council said this:

The council will campaign for changes in existing rent legislation which have left the average rent for controlled tenants at, at the most, twice the 1939 level. This provides a fertile ground for Rachman-type operators to move in with a clear incentive to oust tenants from occu- pation in order to get the full market price for the house.

If this statement is not taken to pieces, a good many people – especially those who do not have to worry about controlled rents – could easily be deceived.

For a start, the basis for increasing controlled rents was the gross value of houses in 1956; and the maximum is now twice that gross value: another third can be claimed if landlords choose to make themselves responsible for indoor decoration; and if they put standard improvements into their houses with the help of a grant, another 12½ per cent of the cost of those improvements can be added to the rent. It is because the average landlord does not choose, no matter for what reason, to do either of these things that the average controlled rent is lower than it could be.

But to go back to those gross values – they are nothing but gross red herrings; and so are those 1939 rent levels. For if the government had allowed landlords to multiply them, not just by two, or two and a third, but by four or six or eight, we would have heard proportionately less protesting about their being out of date. What the landlords' council is saying here, and in a wonderfully roundabout way, is simply that controlled rents are unreasonably low.

But are they? For the poor and elderly inheritor of one or two elderly rent-controlled houses there may be very great hardship because he has no money for repairs and therefore has to forfeit the rent increases allowed since 1957. If the area is one of unemployment he may not easily be able to sell his houses either. But the remedy, there, is that the local authority should either relieve him of his burden or lend him money for repairs. His case is irrelevant to the question of whether maximum controlled rents, where repairs have been done, are still too low. Last September a letter from a prospective London landlord was published in the *Sunday Times*, which neatly punctures this everlasting complaint.

Recently I thought that I might like to buy a second house (on a mortgage) which I would recondition and let at reasonable rentals. When I told the local agents that I aimed to make 10 per cent on property (i.e. 6 per cent to a building society, 4 per cent for myself), they said I was mad or at any rate very naïve. '*Ten per cent is what people make on controlled tenancies,*' they said. 'You could make 25 per cent on bed-sitting rooms standing on your head.'

That letter was published under a one-word heading: 'Greed'. And subsequent inquiries have confirmed that this estimate of 10 per cent profit on rent-controlled property was not exaggerated.

But it is unlikely that the landlords' council would be content with a rise in maximum controlled rents. For that might well be possible without any need to 'campaign for changes in existing rent legislation'. The change they are after, naturally enough, is total decontrol. That is why they blame Rachmanite practices solely on the continued existence of rent control and not on the introduction of creeping or galloping decontrol, or on any of the dozen other contributory causes.

No one can fairly blame landlords, as businessmen, for wanting all restrictions on their liberties removed. And they are certainly not alone – many economists support them – in claiming that houses, like many other goods, should fetch their full market price, which is what the highest bidder will pay for them. But houses are quite unlike any other goods because people need to live in them; and the shortage of them is so acute that the open market prices they now fetch bear no reasonable relation to their rateable values or state of repair. Besides, it should follow, but apparently does not, that if there were a chronic shortage of milk or bread no restrictions should be put on the prices charged for them, and that those who could not pay should go without.

This is exactly what is happening already under partial decontrol, as the tragically mounting problem of homelessness shows. Yet the property owners argue that under total decontrol the situation would somehow right itself or do so in time. Unfortunately there is not the smallest reason why it should.

It is not as if property owners are increasing the number of houses to let for the people of low income, who need them most; and they can scarcely argue that the reason for this has been rent control. For apart from the fact that all new tenancies have been decontrolled for the last seven years, and all but the higher-rated houses too (which means most new houses), those built or converted into flats since 1954 have been free too. In fact, property owners are catering almost exclusively, and on a very small scale, for the renting needs of the rich. Indeed with the price of land as exorbitant as it is – owing to their own speculative machinations – they can now hardly do otherwise and still make what they would consider a worth-while profit. Even non-profit-making housing associations, able to borrow money from the government on easier terms than local authorities, find themselves increasingly unable, even outside London, to provide accommodation, however small, for cost-price rents of less than £4 per week exclusive of rates. And the old houses owned by private landlords which are converted into bed-sitting rooms or flats, at a minimum of 25 per cent profit, are very obviously not for the use of old people now living in rent-controlled houses, but for younger people earning sizeable salaries or possessing private incomes or public grants, who want to escape having to travel long distances to reach their work.

At the same time as the younger childless people, renting singly or in pairs or groups (as grant-aided students so often have to do), are taking up more and more privately owned rentable accommodation, the general stock of it is very rapidly dwindling. More and more people who can afford to do so are buying for their own occupation houses which were once used for letting to at least two families, and are doing so increasingly in villages and in the poorest districts of cities and towns which were once working-class preserves. Again, more and more of these houses are being demolished, either as slums or because they frustrate the insatiable appetites of traffic. So the poorer families of manual workers who need to live near their work are being crammed into less and less privately owned space or squeezed out altogether. And it is in this situation that the property owners are demanding total decontrol of rents and total insecurity of tenure.

What makes this demand so unscrupulous – or, at best, short-sighted – is that it is made in the knowledge that the people who would suffer most are the old people who form the majority of protected tenants, and – to a lesser extent – their sub-tenants (often their own married children who either cannot afford homes of their own or have stayed on to look after their parents). Total decontrol would totally disrupt what remains of interdependent family life, and at enormous cost, financial and otherwise, to the whole community. Where old people on pensions sub-let rooms to married children, they would be put into the invidious position of having most drastically to increase their children's rent by several pounds a week. For in London's industrial districts the typical two-storey 'workman's cottage' now fetches, when decontrolled, anything between £3 and £6 a week for each floor.

How could a widow on a pension and a family with weekly earnings of perhaps £12 a week or less jointly meet rents of this order? Nothing is more likely than that the pensioner would have to get out; and she would have no choice at all in the matter if she lived alone. Of course one could argue that a homeless family could then take over the vacated rooms. But because the incomes of homeless families, in London at any rate, have been found by research rarely to exceed £14 a week, and are often much lower, the incoming tenant would be much more likely to be a childless person on a relatively high salary, or several young adults all contributing their share.

In central London there were already 1,444 homeless families representing 5,640 people in May 1964, and all such figures are minimums because those families who are not accepted for more than a night or two amount to a third more; and in England and Wales there are well over 3,000 children, most of them under five years old, in separate institutions because their parents are homeless. On top of this there are people with children living in coal sheds and disused lorries and parked cars, and families spending nights on bomb-sites and in public lavatories and cafés and workmen's shelters – and, of course, camping on other people's floors. Total decontrol would add to this horror by turning thousands of old people into refugees in their own country. Even with partial decontrol of rents many of them are already in this condition or are existing at semi-starvation level. One old man of nearly eighty was recently found to have nothing but a mattress without sheets or blankets on a damp basement floor while waiting, month after month, for admission to hospital as a cancer patient. The room was one of two, rented for £5 a week by his daughter, and she had no bed or bedding either. Another elderly couple, paying the same rent because they could get nothing cheaper, had £1 a week between them for food and to keep themselves warm. The National Assistance Board – it must be repeated – cannot meet in full rents which it judges unreasonable. And if any other form of rent subsidy were paid direct to tenants of decontrolled private property – with the idea of reducing the very high proportion of their incomes that now has so often to be spent on housing – there would always be a danger of rents being stepped up accordingly by private landlords.

PROPOSALS FOR THE FUTURE

What then is the solution? At times of emergency in the past it has twice been found necessary by governments wedded to free enterprise drastically to control the powers of private landlords. Rent control, with security of tenure, first had to be introduced in 1915 and was imposed again in 1939. The dates are significant. But why should freedom to exploit housing need be curtailed in wartime only? And can anyone seriously hold that we have not got a state of emergency in housing now? While it exists, rent control is the only logical answer. One criticism of it is that it is 'backward-looking'. But freedom to exploit is centuries older. And this criticism is a little one-sided; it never comes from tenants.

Rent control, with its invaluable and essential adjunct of security of tenure, may next time take a slightly different form. It could well be less rigid – this is a personal opinion – with more consideration for the poorly off owner of only one house who needs to get it back to live in it himself. It is unfair that he should be prevented even from claiming simply because he acquired the house after an arbitrarily fixed date.

The level at which rents are controlled could well be related to the state of repair of a house and not just to its rateable value. This is already a consideration when rents of furnished houses are controlled by rent tribunals. It might also be possible to count certain houses as unfurnished, if the standard of furnishing is very poor, and so give their tenants full security, as well as enabling them to bring in their own furniture. Responsibility for house repairs ought, I think, to belong exclusively to house owners; and the onus of making them shoulder it to be transferred from tenants to local authorities. The latter would have to employ many more inspectors, but they need not be fully qualified public health inspectors expert, for instance, on the management of slaughterhouses.

Not all rented houses could, or would, be covered by rent control. Certain types of tenancies would have to be excluded or treated differently, as in the past, because landlords letting rooms in their own houses must have some protection against being saddled interminably with unwelcome tenants, and because some degree of flexibility has to be kept to cater for people with temporary needs.

Incentives for ousting protected tenants, and not only for vacant-possession selling, would therefore still tantalize the wicked landlord. And as a new form of defence for all tenants, every notice to quit should state the reason for giving it and should be made, compulsorily, on a special form which would include a printed note to the tenant telling him that he can consult a solicitor or a Citizens' Advice Bureau. This information has long been included on every summons for debt. A notice to quit not containing it should be counted as invalid. This same information might also be included on the printed forms – giving the terms of tenancy – which landlords should, by rights, stick on to the inside front covers of rent books. Out of the hundreds of rent books I have been shown, not one contained this notice. Its absence should entitle protected tenants to withhold rent. Its presence would remove the need to apply complicated tests for control and decontrol.

These are only two ways of helping to make tenants more aware of the need, and means, of getting advice. But in order to fight malpractices of all kinds, and under whatever changes in tenancy law, we must have much better advisory services.

If Citizens' Advice Bureaux are still to be financially dependent on local authorities (in London, borough councils), the grants made must be much more generous. It is little realized that recent grants from various government departments to the National Council of Social Service have to be spent on setting up new bureaux and on organization generally, or that each bureau has to pay towards the cost of the information supplied to it from headquarters. Probably the public has no idea that because this is a voluntary organization many bureaux, even in London, rely on charities for their office accommodation, and have to be subsidized by them to pay their heavy telephone bills and other running costs and still cannot afford, in spite of a grant from the local authority, to employ a part-time typist, let alone any paid staff. At the moment there are only about 440 bureaux in the whole country (the vast majority of which are entirely run by voluntary workers on a part-time basis). But 'about' is a necessary word because as new bureaux open others have to shut through inability to get staff not needing any pay, of the right quality, and with enough stamina as well as intelligence, for work which could hardly be more useful but which is increasingly responsible, complex, and demanding. A very small minority of bureaux get 100-per-cent grants for their actual needs (as compared with their present running costs), yet where small wartime offices still have to be used and prevent expansion, these needs are often very modest, involving two or three salaries at most.

Possibly local authorities in general do not yet realize what an immense amount of work an expert and properly supported bureau can take over. But the fact remains that in most places we are running a vital preventive service on a shoestring.

It is not much use improving or extending advisory services through which threatened tenants can get help of solicitors if there are not enough solicitors for the job. And in poor districts solicitors are very thin on the ground, especially those operating inexpensive legal advice schemes. Obviously this is not nearly so lucrative as the sort of work on which most solicitors are heavily engaged elsewhere: conveyancing and company law. The result is that the rich are much better served than the poor, and the property owner much better than the tenant – in rather the same way that the private patient is better served than the N.H.S. patient by the medical profession. Those solicitors who are willing to fight for the helpless individual against the big battalions by setting up in the battle area and by accepting every client needing subsidized legal aid clearly get a special satisfaction from this activity which they would not exchange for higher incomes or smarter offices elsewhere. But in the sort of society we have they are counted as quixotic fools; and there may be a case for special financial backing on the evidence of the number of legally aided clients taken and for greater financial advantage in taking them. Too many solicitors who are on the list as willing to give legal advice under the statutory scheme (at 2s. 6d. or free of charge) and under the voluntary scheme at £1 (without a means test) per half-hour session cannot in practice find time to take all who need it.

Because of this shortage of solicitors, the threatened tenant often has no other course but to appeal to the police, who are not allowed to intervene in non-violent tenancy disputes and are not trained to understand the legal rights and wrongs of them – with the frequent and disillusioning result that they either refuse appeals for help or merely give the tenant's family the address of the nearest institution for the homeless.

This difficulty could at least be reduced if the police were empowered to intervene in tenancy disputes if specifically asked to do so by solicitors, Citizens' Advice Bureaux, information officers, or rent tribunal clerks, who would supply them with necessary information. It should be enough for the police to be assured that a tenant is under the protection of a rent tribunal, and will remain so until such and such a date, or that another tenant has not received a valid notice to quit. It is absurd that the police do not even see it as part of their duty to warn threatening landlords that it is unlawful to evict protected tenants without seeking an order from the courts and that to do this to unprotected tenants may land them with heavy damages. Nothing so destroys public confidence in the police as their failure to help the tenant who has the law on his side and can prove it. The fact that they frequently appear in force when blameless tenants of decontrolled property are lawfully evicted does not exactly help matters either.

None of this is the fault of the police themselves. They have their orders. Of course it can be argued that they are understaffed. But if that means that priorities have to be observed it is surely more important to deal with a violent landlord who can make a family homeless than with a motorist who parks for five minutes on the wrong side of the street.

Once a country gets its priorities as hopelessly crossed as that, every sort of social injustice naturally follows, and social chaos becomes almost a foregone conclusion. The fact that the poor family with a need for a secure home is sinking to the bottom of the priority list is not only pitiful but crazy. The work that the father of that family does may be, and usually is, of a kind without which the whole upper structure of wealth and privilege would collapse. By giving landlords a free hand we are pushing out of our cities men who work in the docks, on building sites, in factories, on roads, in public and private transport, in restaurants and hotels, and on every kind of supply and delivery service; and wives who work in hospitals and schools or do the cleaning of offices and shops; we are replacing all these with an army of childless clerical workers and of people who can afford to do no work at all. In London we are even pushing out our doctors, as recent reports of inability to pay high rents for houses with surgery accommodation have shown.

But the exploiting property owner cares nothing about all this. His eyes are so greedily fixed on his short-term profits that he is not even aware that he is a menace to society, let alone that he is cutting the ground from under his own and his children's feet. He will not use his profits to build more rentable housing unless he has a subsidy and a guaranteed rent, and he is now demanding this – as an almost comic sign of the times – without apparently any thought that the taxpayer might prefer his money to go to the non-profit-making producers of houses: local authorities and housing societies. It riles him particularly that millions of pounds have lately been made available to these housing societies; and he fears much more a great council housing drive, belatedly using modern methods of prefabrication, because this is the one way effectively to ease the shortage on which his profits depend. Meanwhile, as well as causing extreme human misery and stepping up the need for higher wages to meet his crippling rents, he has been doing more for extremist political factions than any professional agitator could; and he is bringing the day nearer when, as in other times of national emergency, we may have to resort not only to the requisitioning of houses but to the billetting of homeless families.

If, on the evidence of present damage, the public decides that further decontrol is not acceptable, this will have been inescapably a political decision, for it is on the matter of security for tenants and their families that the two major political parties most sharply diverge. But it would be unfair to expect a Labour government to work miracles overnight. On the contrary, experts have been privately predicting that it would take five years simply to get the present chaotic housing situation under control.

The wicked landlord, however, is not to be exterminated by any superficial means. Put controls on him and he will find ways of slithering round at least some of them. Resist him defensively and he will still get his way with the tenant who is too old or ill or afraid to do anything but give in. Build more houses and he will still turn what remains of the so-called free market into an even blacker one than he has already done. As long as the soil and climate are right for him, as they have been now for so long, his money will buy him acceptance. He will continue to exist – and so will homeless families – as long as land and rented houses remain in private hands.

Facts, Figures, and Estimates

NUMBER OF HOUSES

Total housing stock: 16.5 million approximately.

Houses owned by private landlords: estimates vary between 4 and 5½ million.

AGE OF HOUSES

About 7.6 million houses, i.e. nearly half our housing stock, were built before the First World War, 2.8 million of them before 1862.

UNFIT HOUSES

Number of houses required to replace slum or unfit houses due for clearance in next ten years, plus those which will become obsolete during same period: 500,000 per year

(estimated by Dr E. M. Sigsworth, Lecturer in Economic History, University of York, *The Times*, 24 October 1963).

Number of houses demolished as slums *or* for redevelopment purposes (including road widening), *plus* houses closed in 1962: 64,841

(A house closed *and* demolished in the same year counts as two houses.)

NEW HOUSEHOLDS

In 1961 the Ministry of Housing's chief planner, Mr J. R. James, said that at least 5 million houses would be needed by 1981, 2 million of them for new households.

NEW HOUSES

Total number of houses now being built for private owners and by local authorities: 300,000–350,000 per year

Government target as given in 1964 for total housing production (including replacement of houses demolished, new towns, houses for private owners, etc.): 400,000 houses per year. (This is far below the number required to replace unfit and obsolete houses (see above), let alone all other housing needs, and the *area* in which houses are built is vitally important. So is their price.)

LOCAL AUTHORITY HOUSING, 1954, 1961, 1962

Number of houses, flats, etc. built with subsidy by local authorities as compared with those built for private owners (and therefore not by the government):

	Local Authorities	Private Owners
1954	200,000	88,000
1961	93,000	170,000
1962	105,000	167,000

(Therefore in 1962 privately built houses exceeded publicly built houses by: 62,000.)

Other New Houses Built in 1962

By government departments: 4,700
By housing associations: 1,561

HOUSING NEED

No official figures have ever been available. Waiting lists are no criterion because people register in advance of need and, to a very much greater extent, do not register because there is so little hope. Also, people whose homes are due for clearance do not have to register, nor do those who need to be rehoused on urgent medical grounds. In L.C.C. London applications for the latter have to be made by their doctors. About 1,000 cases have to be deferred every year, and many cannot be rehoused for two years or more. In other big cities the situation is quite as bad.

OVERCROWDING

The 1961 census figures are no real criterion. They are based on the number of people per room, but room-sizes are not taken into account. It has recently been estimated that about one in five families are overcrowded. In Birmingham alone 38,000 people live in houses in multiple occupation (*The Times*, 3 December 1962).

LIVING STANDARDS

An analysis made by the Labour Research Department on the results of the 1961 census runs as follows:

Of the 10½ million households so far covered, no less than 3.3 million – or nearly one family in three – lack exclusive use of one or more of the four household arrangements necessary for decent living standards – an indoor water-closet, hot and cold water, a fixed bath.

According to the same source 589,000 families are without a w.c. either in the building or attached to it. And the report continues by explaining that in towns this means using a w.c. in a yard or back garden which may be some distance from the house and may be shared with other families.

In both Leeds and Sheffield round about one fifth of the households live in this way. Indeed the overwhelming majority of houses without water closets in the West Riding are in towns and not in rural areas.

PRICES AND RENTS

Increase in the price of old houses over the last 5 years: 60%
  „   „   new   „   „   :   40%
Present average price of houses for sale in London as given in March 1964 by Mrs Christine Cockburn, London School of Economics: over £4,000

An Example of Inflated Land Values in London. In January 1964 four properties and a courtyard occupying 11,000 square feet in Mayfair (about a quarter of an acre) changed hands at £500,000, or £2 million per acre (reported in the *Evening Standard*, 24 January 1964).

AN EXAMPLE OF GAINS BY PRIVATE LANDLORDS FROM DE-CONTROL UNDER THE 1957 RENT ACT

The rental income of Greencoat Properties rose from £134,000 p.a. before the Rent Act, to £385,000 in 1962 (as stated by the Labour Research Department).

RISING RENTS IN CENTRAL LONDON

Research undertaken by the London School of Economics for

the Rowntree Trust has shown that in the borough of St Marylebone rents doubled between 1958 and 1961. Among the new tenants not one was a manual worker.

SUBSIDIES AND MORTGAGES

'The existing Exchequer subsidy to council tenants is no higher than the tax relief granted to owner-occupiers paying the standard rate of tax. It is very much lower than the tax relief given to owners who pay surtax', Della Adam Nevitt, Senior Research Officer, London School of Economics, in the *Guardian*, 1963.

IMPROVEMENT GRANTS

In February 1964 Mr A. Evans, M.P., said in the House of Commons that under proposed legislation a property company owning 100 decontrolled houses could get £30,000 of public money in the form of improvement grants and after only three years would be free to sell the houses.

CREEPING DECONTROL

Unfurnished tenancies in privately owned property: rate at which these were becoming decontrolled on a change of tenancy, i.e. by creeping decontrol, in England and Wales (excluding business premises) in 1959:   320,000 per year
(This is the latest official figure available.)

DECONTROL BY RATEABLE VALUE

Government estimate of the number of units of accommodation which would become decontrolled when the 1957 Rent Act came into force by virtue of their rateable value: 750,000.
Actual number just under 400,000.
This striking overestimate was due to insufficient research.

EFFECT OF THE 1957 RENT ACT ON OVERCROWDING

The government's survey of the effects of the Rent Act also showed that the expected shift from overcrowded accommodation into underoccupied accommodation had not taken place. In fact, the number of underoccupied units had increased.

REPAIRS

The government's report published in 1960 showed that the machinery designed for the use of tenants of rent-controlled property had been working very unsatisfactorily. For instance in Metropolitan London 80 per cent of tenants who had sent in Form G (requesting repairs) 'had never received an undertaking from the landlord to do the repairs', and of these 'only 15 per cent had a certificate of disrepair'. The rent aspect was even more deplorable, as shown in the final sentences of the report:

In as many as half the cases where the tenant said that the landlord's undertaking on Form H had not been honoured the rent had not been reduced. The difficulty in these cases may have been that the tenant, although entitled to proceed as if a certificate of disrepair existed, had not got one. It was however surprising to find no rent reduction in a fifth of the cases where a current certificate of disrepair was in force.

RENT TRIBUNALS

Number of new applications received during 1962   6,169

COST OF LAND FOR HOUSING IN LONDON

Cost of land bought by the L.C.C. for housing in 1951: £8,800 per acre.

Cost of land bought by the L.C.C. for housing in 1964: £618,800 per acre.

A 12-acre site recently bought by Enfield Corporation for £240,000 had cost the vendor only £7,500 three years before (*Hansard*, 15 July 1964).

NATIONAL ASSISTANCE, 1962

Rent Allowances. Number of tenants on weekly allowances paying rent (plus rates) to landlords other than local authorities
767,000

Number of cases where rent was £2 10s. or more (but below £7 p.w.)   50,000

Number of cases where rent was considered 'not reasonable in the circumstances' and not met in full   31,000

Age and Status. Of the 31,000 tenants allowed less than the full amount of their rent, nearly 11,000 were over pension age, and a high proportion were men or women living alone (more than 50 per cent of the total). About another 10 per cent of the total were 'married couples without children', but this does not mean that all of them were childless – in some cases it could mean that the children were elsewhere, for instance in public care due to homelessness. Therefore the number of families with children affected – rather less than 9,000 – is a little misleading.

The Wage-Stop. This applies exclusively to families with children. In 1962 the number of unemployed men with dependent children was 77,000, and the number of such families who received a cut rate of assistance, due to the wage-stop, was 25,000. The average assistance allowance resulting from the cuts was £8 a week – or less than half of average industrial earnings. As the cuts are designed to reduce the incomes of assisted families to just below the level of their fathers' net earnings in full-time work, such earnings could not have averaged more than just over £8 a week. Big families on full assistance would normally be entitled to more, and often much more, than £8 p.w. because, in addition to an allowance for rent, the scale rate for a married couple is £5 4s. 6d. p.w. and the rates for children average just over £1 per head. The biggest, and previously lowest-earning, families are therefore liable to the heaviest cuts in assistance.

In 1962, out of the 77,000 unemployed families with dependent children, 13,000 had five or more children. But 11,000 had no more than four children; and the highest number quoted by the N.A.B. in this context, 15,000, had only three children – the other 38,000 having fewer. A factor which, as a matter of observation, is making an increasing number of the smaller families liable to the wage-stop is rising rents: a rent of £3 a week, allowed in full by the N.A.B., is equivalent to allowances for three young children.

1962 was a year of abnormally high unemployment but, with rising rents, the *proportion* of wage-stopped families is likely to increase still further. Recently, men unable to work through *illness* (and receiving sickness benefit) have found themselves and their families wage-stopped.

THE COST OF HOMELESSNESS

In 1961 there were roughly 1,000 children in the care of the London County Council – either in children's homes or boarded out with foster parents – because their own parents were homeless. The cost of this was about £½ million per year. The cost for each child was twice that of providing a new L.C.C. flat, or house. The cost of keeping a homeless mother and two children in the poorest type of reception centre is £17 p.w. The fact that, outside central London, all such costs are lower does not alter the basic paradox.

HOUSING ASSOCIATIONS AND HOMELESSNESS

Several voluntary housing associations have recently been formed for buying old houses in which homeless families (usually chosen from those already in reception centres) can rent rooms or flats. Addresses from the National Federation of Housing Societies, 12 Suffolk St, London sw1, or from the fund-raising body, Christian Action, 1 Amen Court, London ec4.

PREVENTING HOMELESSNESS UNDER THE CHILDREN AND YOUNG PERSONS ACT 1963

Under this Act local authorities have a duty to make 'advice, guidance, and assistance' – if necessary, in cash – available in order to prevent children from having to go into public care. This help in cash has not so far been available to prevent homelessness where children would go into reception centres with their mothers – as in L.C.C. London.

The need for regular help with cash is naturally very great among families without a full-time wage-earner who have been on National Assistance for months or years, rather than weeks, and most particularly among those who are on cut rates of assistance (see above). The Act took no account of the formidable difficulties involved in giving regular cash help to State-assisted families. Even where the wage-stop or similar policies are not in operation, the maximum weekly sum provided from any single outside source which the N.A.B. can disregard is only 15s. per week, no matter how many children there are, nor whether the family has just suffered a knockout blow such as the death, departure, or disablement of one of the parents – and irrespective also of the existence or otherwise of crippling commitments.

After the passing of the 1963 Act it was found necessary to point out, officially and for the first time, these financial obstacles to the prevention of homelessness and the separation of children from their parents. Yet they had existed for sixteen years.

Tenants' Check List